Parent Power

Bringing up Responsible Children and Teenagers

John Sharry

JOHN WILEY & SONS, LTD

First published by Veritas as
Bringing up Responsible Children (1999)
and
Bringing up Responsible Teenagers (2001)

Copyright © 2002 by John Wiley & Sons, Ltd,
The Atrium, Southern Gate, Chichester,
West Sussex PO19 8SQ, England

Telephone (+44) 1243 779777
e-mail (for orders and customer service enquiries):
cs-books@wiley.co.uk
Visit our Home Page on http://www.wileyeurope.co.uk
or http://www.wiley.com

This publication is designed to provide accurate and authoritative information in regard to the subject matter covered. It is sold on the understanding that the Publisher is not engaged in rendering professional services. If professional advice or other expert assistance is required, the services of a competent professional should be sought.

Other Wiley Editorial Offices

John Wiley & Sons, Inc., 111 River Street, Hoboken, NJ 07030, USA

Jossey-Bass, 989 Market Street, San Francisco, CA 94103-1741, USA

WILEY-VCH Verlag GmbH, Boschstr. 12, D-69469 Weinheim, Germany

John Wiley & Sons Australia, Ltd, 33 Park Road, Milton, Queensland 4064, Australia

John Wiley & Sons (Asia) Pte, Ltd, 2 Clementi Loop #02-01, Jin Xing Distripark, Singapore 129809

John Wiley & Sons Canada Ltd, 22 Worcester Road, Etobicoke, Ontario M9W 1L1, Canada

Cartoons by John Byrne

Library of Congress Cataloging-in-Publication Data
A catalogue record for this book has been requested

British Library Cataloguing in Publication Data
A catalogue record for this book is available from the British Library

ISBN 0-470-85023-X

Project management by Originator, Gt Yarmouth, Norfolk (typeset in 11.5/13pt Imprint)
Printed and bound in Great Britain by Biddles Ltd, Guildford and King's Lynn
This book is printed on acid-free paper responsibly manufactured from sustainable forestry, in which at least two trees are planted for each one used for paper production.

This book is dedicated to the hundreds of parents, children and teenagers I have had the privilege to work with over the years. Their creativity and spirit in the face of problems has always been a great inspiration to me. They have taught me all I know about good parenting and it is from their knowledge that this book is primarily written. I hope it does justice in communicating their struggles, their triumphs and above all their wisdom.

Contents

viii   Contents

About the author

Dr John Sharry is a psychotherapist and principal social worker at the Department of Child and Family Psychiatry, Mater Hospital, as well as a director of the Brief Therapy Group in Dublin. He has co-written the Parents Plus Programmes (video-based parenting guides) and several self-help books for parents including *Bringing up Responsible Children* (1999), *Bringing up Responsible Teenagers* (2001) and *When Parents Separate* (2001), all published by Veritas. His practice website is www.brieftherapy.ie

INTRODUCTION

Parenting – a roller coaster ride

Being a parent is like being on a roller coaster. Once you get on, there is no getting off and you never know what is coming round the next corner. There are loads of ups and downs, lots of highs and

lows. The ride can make you so frightened, scared and sick as well as thrilled, excited and delighted – all at the same time! But like being on a roller coaster, it is the ups and downs that make it so wonderful. The most important thing is to 'go with the flow', do your best to hang on and to let yourself enjoy the experience.

One of my favourite films is *Parenthood* starring Steve Martin. The film provides a sympathetic and humorous look at the joys and challenges of being a parent and of family life in general. The central character, Steve Martin, struggles to be a good father, different from his own father who was not there for him, only to find himself making many of the same errors. A turning point in the film is when his grandmother uses the metaphor of a roller coaster ride to explain what parenting is all about. He begins to accept the unpredictable nature of being a parent, realising that many of the 'ups and downs' bring the most meaning and fulfilment. This shift in thinking allows him to let go of his worries, to simply do his best and to enjoy the experience. It also helps him become more compassionate towards himself as a parent, more accepting of his children as they are and more forgiving towards his own father. In this book, I attempt to promote a compassionate look at parenting and family life. My aim is to support you as you carry out a difficult but very valuable job. I hope to encourage you to enjoy the ups and downs of what is certainly a roller coaster ride!

The challenges of parenting

With increased pressures on families, being a parent these days can be a difficult task. With less support from extended family and the community, families sometimes feel more isolated than they did in the past. In addition there is the scrutiny from outside: there is much debate as to what is good parenting, and bigger expectations for parents to achieve this. We are much more aware of the need of children to receive unconditional love and affirmation and how this is vital for them to grow up into happy, confident and independent adults. Yet we are also aware of the dangers of over-liberal parenting, and none of us wants our children to be spoiled or out of control.

Many parents are confused as to what is the best way to discipline children. Many of the authoritarian means of discipline (such as physical punishment) which we were brought up with are being increasingly questioned. Yet there is little information on effective alternatives. Often being responsible and being loving as a parent seem to be in contradiction. How can parents maintain a good and loving relationship with their children while also teaching what is right and wrong and helping them learn good social behaviour?

This book attempts to provide an answer to this question, by describing a 'middle way' approach to parenting that shows how you can positively encourage children to behave well, teaching them how to take responsibility for their actions, while also maintaining a satisfying and enjoyable relationship with them. The long-term aim is to help your children grow into responsible adults who are independent and confident but also appropriately connected to their family and able to form their own intimate relationships in the future.

Empowering parenting

Many writers describe family life as being like embarking on a plane journey together.* You start the journey with a destination in mind and a navigation plan, but throughout the journey you can get thrown off course by other factors such as wind or rain or other air traffic. Being off course is in fact quite normal. As Stephen Covey says, 'Good families – even great families – are off track 90 percent of the time!' What matters most, is that you keep returning to your original course, you keep the destination in mind. You don't let events throw you off course permanently and you keep returning to the flight plan.

The metaphor of a plane journey is also a good one to

---

* See Nelson and Lott (2000, p. 369) and Covey (1997, p. 367) – both listed in 'Further Reading' at the back of the book.

describe the long-term aim of parenting. When a child is born the parent is in the pilot's seat and is very much in charge of the controls. Parents make all the decisions about infants and young children's lives, about what they wear and where they go, etc. As a child begins to get older, a good parent allows the child into the cockpit and begins to teach him how to operate the controls. The child begins to make some decisions for himself and learns how to do some flying under the supervision of the parent. As the child becomes a teenager, he begins to take the first steps of flying his own plane.

As a parent your role is really one of 'co-pilot'. Over the years your aim is to slowly teach your children all they need to become confident, independent and responsible adults. Your goal is to patiently teach them all the skills they will need to fly their own plane. A good 'co-pilot' is there for their children and teenagers, offering encouragement and guidance, letting them learn from mistakes and achievements, and handing over one by one the responsibilities of being an independent adult.

This training process is often difficult for families. Many parents fear that their children will not be able to fly safely and they battle with their children to take back the controls, insisting that they take over the flying. Other parents are critical and undermining of their children's

ability to fly and they never release them to fly in the first place. And other parents do not give children any lessons at all, letting them learn the skills of flying from other people, such as their school friends or from the television. Good parents, however, realise that the aim of the journey is not for the parent to remain in the cockpit, but to teach their children how to fly their own planes. They realise that it is far better for children to learn the vital task of being an adult, with their parents acting as good co-pilots – present, involved and supportive of them. A good co-pilot has faith in the trainee pilot's ability and is there actively to encourage them in the crucial job of flying the plane.

How to use this book

This book is divided into two parts: (1) Parenting young children from three to age eleven and (2) Parenting teenagers. Clearly there is overlap between the two parts and many of the ideas are interchangeable. For example, Steps 5–8 in Part 2 focus on resolving conflict and negotiating agreements and this clearly can work with children as young as eight as well as teenagers. Equally, many of the ideas in Part 1, such as those on rewards, sanctions, effective commands and even time out, can be applied with young teenagers. Certainly if your child is ten or eleven years old then both parts of the book might be equally relevant.

In addition, each part of the book is divided between eight well-researched principles of parenting which are derived from two parenting courses (the Parents Plus Children's Programme and the Parents Plus Adolescents' Programme) which were developed in Ireland.

The principles in the book are less concerned with

finding a cause for why things go wrong in families or for why children have problems and more interested in helping parents to find solutions to these problems and to create more satisfying ways of relating to their children. The focus is on the interaction between parent and child – when parents respond differently to their children, they help their children behave differently. The goal is to help parents discover ways of communicating (many of which you will be using already) with their children that are positive and which in turn help children and teenagers to change positively.

The principles in the two parts of the book can be viewed as eight steps that you can follow one by one over the next few weeks. Most of the ideas will be familiar to you and be recognised as good, positive habits of parenting to which we all aspire. While the ideas are well researched as useful to most families, none apply in every situation and in every context. Each parent, each child and each family is different, and it is the parents who know their children and their families best. Rather than giving you ready-made solutions, the aim of this book is to encourage you to pause and reflect about your parenting and to discover what works for you with your children. I invite you to adapt the ideas and suggestions provided in the book to your own unique family situation. While I encourage you to try new things out, trust your own gut instinct to lead you to what's best for you and your family.

Who the book is for

This book is for anybody who has a responsibility to care for children and teenagers. This includes fathers, mothers, foster parents, step-parents, grandparents,

even uncles and aunts and anybody else who has a responsibility to provide nurturing and guidance to a child
or teenager, either on a full-time or a part-time basis.
Throughout the book, I use the word parent, but you
can substitute the word grandparent or foster parent or
any other one, if these more accurately describe your
situation. Equally, when I use the word family throughout
the book I want to include all types of families including
separated families, stepfamilies, single-parent families
and blended families. Throughout the book I have used
a number of case studies that I hope are representative of
the different types of families I have worked with. I have
alternated between girls and boys and male and female
parents in order to be as inclusive as possible. I hope the
ideas can be of benefit to you in whatever context you find
yourself.

Build on your strengths as a parent

You will notice that, throughout this book, I encourage
you to build on your children's strengths and abilities.
I also encourage you to apply the same principles to
yourself. Too often parents give themselves a hard time,
criticising their own behaviour and putting themselves
down. Too often they focus on what they do wrong in

every situation, thinking 'I wish I hadn't lost my patience like that', or 'I should have more time for my children'. Similarly, parents in couple relationships can relate negatively to each other, focusing on what the other has done wrong: 'I don't like the way you interrupted me talking to the kids', or 'You shouldn't have lost your temper then'.

I encourage you to break this negative pattern and reverse it. Start looking for what you and your partner are doing right as parents. Be on the lookout for the small steps of improvement you make each day, the times you manage successfully. Begin to notice what you like about yourself as a parent. Don't be afraid to praise yourself: 'I'm pleased at how I was firm in that instance', or 'I'm glad that at least I tried my best'. Equally, if you are part of a couple, be on the lookout for examples of behaviour you like in your partner: 'Thanks for supporting me with Joe like that', or 'I'm really pleased that you came home early and we have some time to ourselves'.

It is in your children's interests for you to identify your own strengths and successes. Children learn a powerful lesson from you when you model self-encouragement. They learn how to be confident and successful and how to relate positively to other people.

Often parents go through difficult periods when it is hard for them to be consistent or to give their children all

MUM, DAD - THE ONE THING I'VE LEARNED FROM YOU MOST IS SELF ENCOURAGEMENT.

THANKS - THAT'S VERY ENCOURAGING.

the time they deserve. At times like these, the worst thing parents can do is excessively blame themselves or be over-defensive. It is better to try to learn from the experience, acknowledge what needs to be done differently and move on. Self-compassion is as important as compassion toward others. It is powerful modelling for children to see their parents being honest about their mistakes and not dwelling on them but moving on to make a fresh start. This helps children learn how to move on from misbehaviour in the same way.

Remember, the goal is not to be a perfect parent or to have a perfect child. Such people do not exist (and if they did they would be unbearable to be around!). Rather, the goal is to be a 'good enough' parent – someone who accepts themselves as good enough, appreciates their own strengths as well as their weaknesses, tries their best and learns from experience.

Start with caring for yourself

Unfortunately, many of the parents I meet are stressed and 'burnt out'. They have put all their energies into caring for and attending to their children, so much so that there is little time and attention for themselves.

While their intentions are admirable, the long-term results are bad for themselves and their children. If you are burnt out and stressed, you can no longer be there for your children; you can even become negative, inconsistent and resentful in your parenting. So you really have to turn this around and start with yourself.

The first suggestion I give to stressed parents is that they try and turn some of the care and attention that they have lavished on their children towards themselves. I suggest that they take time to identify and think about their own needs and wants and then decide to prioritise and care for themselves as well as their children. The irony is that such a switch to self-care benefits their children as much as themselves, as the children will have access to more content, positive and resourced parents than before. Most of this book is about ways of providing positive attention and care to children and teenagers whether this is by praise, encouragement, rewards or respectful listening and communication. The first step, however, is really to make sure we treat ourselves the same way!

Tips for going forward

1   Set aside some time next week, to identify your needs and wishes as a person and as a parent.

2   Plan a special time for yourself in the next week, doing something you really enjoy.

3   Promise to think positively about yourself over the next week. Look for examples of your good parenting.

Pausing to think about your parenting

Eight-year-old Pete and his six-year-old brother were constantly squabbling and rowing. Their mother Julie would never get a moment's peace before one of them would approach her complaining that the other had hit him or taken his toy or been nasty to him. She found herself getting drawn into their rows trying to 'be the referee' deciding who was right and who was wrong. But this would lead to protests and tears, particularly by Pete who always felt wronged. She often found herself becoming angry and frustrated and this would leave her stressed for the day.

When faced by a conflict or a difficult situation we can find ourselves immediately reacting in a certain way without too much thought or deliberation. Sometimes our immediate reactions are helpful, for example, when we naturally respond to soothe a child who is crying in distress. But other times they can be unhelpful, for

SINCE I LEARNED TO PRESS MY 'PAUSE' BUTTON, THE STORY'S GOT A MUCH HAPPIER ENDING.

example if we react over-angrily to a minor challenge from one of our children or if we say something damaging in the heat of a row. Many different things determine how we react to other people and our children. It can be simply a habit (good or bad) that we have developed over the years or it can be a repetition of how we were treated by our own parents in the past, or it can be a function of how stressed or strongly we feel about what is currently happening. In addition, we all have our specific weaknesses; we all have our 'buttons' that when pressed by others make us fly off the handle.

Problems can occur, however, when we get stuck in our reactions or when they become over-rigid and negative. Most problems in families are maintained by patterns of reactions between parents and children that have become fixed over time. In the example above, the fact that Julie jumps in and becomes the referee each time her children squabble may be part of the problem. Maybe getting drawn into an argument about who was right and who was wrong only intensifies the problem.

So how can you break these cycles of reacting? How can you break the patterns of the problem? The first thing you can do is to pause and to take time to think about what is going on. Rather than letting your children 'press your fast-forward button' you decide to press 'pause', so you can begin to choose how you best want to respond. Consider now how Julie, the mother in the opening example of this chapter, paused and thought through how she wanted to respond to the problem she was facing:

When Julie took time to think about her sons' squabbles she wondered if it had simply become a way for them to get her attention and that it had simply become a habit for her to drop everything and get involved. Thinking about it, she also realised that in the role of referee she generally took the side of the younger boy, which was probably unfair as they were both responsible.

Julie realised that she did not want her sons to be dependent on her to sort out every squabble and wanted to teach them to sort things out themselves. She was also unhappy with the way she was acting angrily in the argument (which clearly wasn't working) and she wanted to find a calmer more respectful way to help her sons sort this problem out.

So Julie made some decisions. (1) Instead of jumping in to referee when her two sons got into a squabble, she decided to back off, saying to them, 'Listen, the two of you are old enough to sort your disagreements out'. (2) If the squabble escalated and she had to intervene, she would not be the judge or referee, but would firmly and calmly tell the children that they had to take time apart for a few minutes (or the disputed toy would be taken away) until they could play better together. (3) Julie resolved also to talk things through with her sons at a later time, when they were calmer, about how they could get on better together.

Pausing to solve problems

Family and child problems are commonplace. Good
families, even great families, all experience problems.
All parents are challenged deeply at times by one or
more of their children and all parents find themselves
reacting in ways or saying things that on reflection, they
wish they hadn't. The mark of a healthy family is not
whether they have problems or not, but how they
respond to the problems they have. Healthy families do
let problems overwhelm them and take active steps to try
and solve and manage them better. Pausing to think
through how to respond to problems is generally the
first step to solving problems, even quite serious ones.
Furthermore, this gives you the satisfaction of taking
control of your own reactions and being able to choose a
more respectful and empowering response to what is happening. In later chapters, we will look at how you can use
these principles to sit down with your children and/or
your partner to solve problems; but even if others are
not yet participating, you can decide to take a lead yourself. You can decide that you are going to first pause and
think through what way you want to respond.

Consider the following principles to help you think
through how you want to respond to problems:

1 Think carefully about what is really going on during
the problem.

Is your child looking for attention or is she feeling inadequate? Is it a power struggle between you? Is it caused by your own unrealistic expectations? Some honest self-reflection is called for.

2 Focus on your goal and what you want to achieve.
   What do you want to happen? What do your children want to happen? How can you get both goals met? For example, your child may want to stay out with friends and you want them to spend more time at home. Perhaps you could get to know some of their friends and arrange for them to come over to your house.

3 Think of what way you want to respond.
   Most parents I meet are deeply unhappy when they find themselves reacting angrily or negatively to their children. Even if the problem is not immediately reduced, you are more likely to feel happier in yourself if you respond calmly, respectfully and more patiently.

4 Focus on what you can do.
   Rather than waiting for your child to change first, what can you do to help her change or to make the situation better?

5 Remember what has worked with your child in the past.
   For example, one parent realised that it was a 'bad time' to harangue his daughter with questions about how school went the minute she came in from school and was tired, and remembered that a better time was later, after dinner, when everyone was relaxed.

6 If something isn't working, try something different.
   For example, if nagging doesn't work, try backing

off and giving your children some space to decide for themselves. Be prepared to have to try out a few different responses or to think about things several times before you find what works for you and your child.

Pausing for a change – more examples

SAYING 'NO'

Jean's five-year-old son would always say 'No' when she asked him to do simple things like tidying up. This would annoy Jean greatly and she would react in an authoritarian manner, insisting her son did what she said. Her son would then react angrily and 'dig his heels in' and a long power struggle would take place between them, setting a very bad tone for the rest of the day.

When Jean took some time out to think about what was happening, talking the problem through with a friend of hers, she realised that the battle of wills between them was making things worse. She realised that her young son found it very hard for him to be 'told what to do' and rebelled if she was angry or argumentative in her style

of insisting. As a result she decided in the first place to acknowledge his feelings in a respectful way, *without giving in or getting drawn into an argument*, when she had to insist on something being done. For example, she would say, 'I know you'd like to stay playing now, but we have to tidy up now for dinner ... you'll be able to play later after dinner'. Then, in the second place, she'd give her son choices whenever possible so he could take some control. For example, she might say, 'Would you like me to help you tidy up?', or 'Which game will we tidy away first?'. This respectful cooperative approach helped reduce a lot of the power struggles between them.

LEAVING A MESS

Peter used to constantly nag his thirteen-year-old daughter not to leave her 'stuff all over the house' and to clean her room which was like a 'pigsty'. The problem continued and it was a constant source of tension between them leading to big public rows about it. When he paused to think about it, Peter realised that, while the house being clean was a big issue for him, the most important thing was the relationship with his daughter which was suffering because of the nagging and conflict. As a result he chose a good time to talk the problem through with her. The conversation took place when he was driving her to a class, which worked well as they had privacy and no interruptions. When he listened she told him how much it bothered her that he was on her back all the time and how it hurt her that he criticised her in front of other people. They reached a compromise about the cleaning. She resolved to make sure none of her stuff was in the communal areas of the house, and he resolved to back off and let her take responsibility for her room. The arrangement worked reasonably well, and they were able to

joke a little about it. But most importantly, the fact they
had spoken about it, heard each other's point of view and
come to an agreement had cleared the air and made a big
difference, improving their relationship.

DAWDLING AT HOMEWORK

James's eight-year-old son, Tony, would dawdle and
delay doing his homework as James sat with him. He
would slowly do his writing and pretend he didn't know
how to do his sums. James had to 'sit over him' as he did
each part of his homework and he became increasingly
frustrated as it would take longer and longer, and it
really delayed him getting the dinner ready. Often
James would end up nagging him and this would eventually lead to a row.

When James paused to think about what was going on,
he realised that he had high expectations about his son's
abilities, when in fact his son might be struggling with the
work. He also realised that sitting over his son and turning
homework into a battleground might be further undermining his confidence about what he could do. As a
result, James made contact with Tony's teacher and together they came up with a plan as to how to help his son,
which included less, but more focused, homework and a
referral for help from the remedial teacher. James also
changed his style of helping Tony at homework. He set
aside a fixed homework time during which Tony was to
try his best to get everything done. James only sat with
Tony at the beginning and end of homework, ensuring
that Tony had a lot of time to try out the work himself.
In addition, James became very positive, picking out what
Tony had done well rather than what he had done wrong.
He also focused on helping Tony improve at his own pace.
Finally, James made sure that a period of playtime

followed homework as a natural reward to Tony for all his work.

ALL STRESSED OUT

Joe worked in a very high-powered job that placed great demands on him. When he came home to his wife and children, he would be frequently preoccupied and stressed. Often he would be grumpy and snap angrily at his children over minor things. He used to collapse in front of the TV and not even have time to play with them. When he had time away, Joe began to reflect on how out-of-balance his life had become. He realised that his family and children were more important than his work and wanted to spend more time with them. As a result he began to change his working hours, trying to get home earlier. A useful routine he found was to take a fifteen-minute walk through the park before he went home. During this time to himself, he would unwind and let the stress of the day go. He would prepare himself to arrive home, pleasant and attentive to his children who would be demanding his attention.

Nothing works all the time or for everybody

I hope reading this book will give you a chance to 'pause' and reflect about your parenting. By taking time to think through what was really going on, you can come up with a respectful response that has a good chance of working. While you can't control how your children will react, what you can do is change your own responses. And what you will find is that, when you can choose respectful and empowering responses taking into account your own and your child's needs (rather than reacting the same way over and over again), you will begin to positively influence your children. In simple terms, your children will begin to change as you begin to change. It is important to remember, however, that nothing works all the time or for everybody or in every situation. For example, in some situations ignoring a child's tantrum can cause too much distress and it can be better to adopt a more soothing or listening approach. What counts is that you take time to think through what works for you, and that you are flexible enough to adapt and change if something is not working. You may have to 'press the pause button' several times before you finally work out how best to manage a problem!

Tips for going forward

1 Think of a particular problem that occurs in your family. Take some time to think it through until you understand what is going on and what you might do differently to make a difference.

2 Sit down and make a list of your goals. What way do you want to be as a parent, as a couple (if you have a partner), as a family? What is important? Maybe start a discussion with others in the family.

PART 1

BEING A PARENT OF A YOUNG CHILD

Providing positive attention to children

Bedtime with four-year-old Zoe was a nightmare. She just would not settle by herself and would insist on story after story from her parents. First, she wanted her Dad to read and then her Mum. When they left her, she would cry until they came back or she would come down the stairs saying she was thirsty or the room was too cold or too hot. Her parents would go up to sort this out and then she would want something else. It was endless. Her parents would resort to lecturing, cajoling and bribing her to stay in her room, with just 'one more story' or 'another five minutes downstairs'. Both her parents and Zoe herself would become exhausted and sometimes very upset.

Have you noticed how young children will do anything to get their parents' attention? Having their parents notice and respond to them is probably the greatest reward for children and they will seek this in as many ways as possible. Often parents find ways of giving approving, loving attention to their children, with warm hugs, close conversations and kind words. These are good habits and are very healthy for parent and child. Unfortunately, parents often unwittingly provide attention negatively via shouting, criticising and even slapping. Strange as it may seem, these negative interactions are preferable to no attention at all and children will seek them out in place of being ignored.

In the example above, Zoe is getting loads of attention from her parents for *not going to bed*. If she makes a fuss she gets extra stories, extra time up and can even persuade her parents to sit in the bed with her. You'd wonder why she would want to change this at all! In this situation her parents can make some simple changes in how they respond to Zoe at night time that could make a real difference. For example, they could

1 Set up a routine at night (which they keep!) that specifies at what time she goes to bed, how many stories she gets, and at what time they leave her in her room.

2 Ensure she gets lots of positive attention during the stories and lots of praise when she goes to bed on time, or gets into the bed as asked.

3 Ensure she gets little attention when she gets out of bed or asks for something. The parents could firmly guide her back to her bed, without saying much at all.

4 Ensure she gets no extra rewards such as an extra story or extra time up, when she gets out of the bed, but is simply brought back to her room.

5 Also use a star chart to encourage her to stay in her bed (see Step 4 for information on star charts).

Catch your child being good

We know from research that when attention is given to a certain behaviour, that behaviour tends to be repeated and to develop, while behaviour that is not given attention disappears. It is human nature to get trapped into giving children more attention when they are misbehaving than when they are behaving well. For example, when two children are playing quietly together they are usually ignored until one of them starts an argument or begins whining. Parents respond rapidly to the child's negative behaviour, often with criticism or scolding, thus providing attention for negative behaviour while ignoring the positive behaviour shown when the children were playing quietly. If this pattern is repeated often enough, it does not take long for children to learn from experience that fighting and whining get a lot of adult attention. Sometimes this can become a vicious cycle. A child who misbehaves gains attention from a parent in the form of shouting or criticising. This can leave both parent and child upset and angry. From this position the child is more likely to seek attention again with misbehaviour

and the parent more likely to respond angrily, and so the cycle repeats itself.

So how can you break this cycle? Or, even better, how can you turn it on its head so that it becomes a positive cycle? The best way to do this is to go out of your way to make sure your children get lots of positive attention and encouragement whenever they behave well – literally catch your child being good. This positive attention leaves both you and your child feeling more content and close to one another. From this position the child is more likely to seek attention positively by behaving well again and the parent is more likely to respond positively. Thus this new positive cycle is established.

It can be difficult to make this switch to positive attention, especially when you are not used to it, or if you have experienced a lot of difficult behaviour in the past. However, it can make a real difference if you give it a try, and let go of any resentment from past misbehaviour. Consider the example of Robin:

Robin had been involved in a lot of conflict with her ten-year-old son, usually on a daily basis. This usually started with him refusing to get out of bed in the morning, while she repeatedly called him with increasing irritation, ending in a screaming match, which set the scene for the rest of the day. Almost every interaction between them until the end of the day was hostile and negative. When Robin first started a parenting course, desperate to change things, she couldn't imagine being able to find anything good about her son's behaviour to which she could pay positive attention.

However, when she stood back a bit from the situation and observed her son, she quickly saw that there were many previously unnoticed aspects of his behaviour which she could acknowledge with positive attention. When he brought his cup over to the sink after breakfast she smiled and thanked him. When he let his younger brother play a computer game with him she said, 'It's very nice the way you are kind to your brother'. When he sat down to do his homework, she was able to comment positively on this. Over time she began to see more and more things that she could praise and encourage and she began to enjoy the change of approach and how it made her feel different. Her son's behaviour changed positively over a number of months and the relationship between them improved markedly.

How to give positive attention

Going out of our way to give positive attention can feel a little uncomfortable at first – in our culture we are not used to it. But it gets easier and feels more natural as you persist with it and find your own individual style.

There is no one right way to provide positive attention. What is most important is that it is personal and experienced as genuine by both parent and child. With young children, a simple pat on the head or a warm smile can be enough. For older children you may want to specifically comment on the behaviour you like. For example, you could say, 'I see you've started your homework, that's good', or 'I'm really pleased to see that you've come in on time'.

If you are used to a lot of difficult behaviour from your child and feel there is little you can notice that is positive, a good way to get started is to spend some time thinking about the things you like about your child. You might want to recall the times he or she behaved well in the past (however long ago!) or times you enjoyed together and felt close. When you have pictured some of these things in your mind, write down one or two of them. When you've made a list, keep it in a safe place, and over the next few days look for further things your child does that you like and begin to note these down also. As you collect more and more examples of good behaviour, your attitude toward your child will change. Then, when you're ready, you can share some of your observations with your child. By now you are giving some really good positive attention to him or her.

Positive attention can divert misbehaviour

Psychologists have found that much of children's misbehaviour is rewarded by the attention it receives. They have also found that a bout of misbehaviour often happens just after a period of good behaviour that has gone unnoticed. By attending to the good behaviour first you can give children the attention they are looking for and divert them from seeking the attention negatively. A good example of this comes from a time I was working with a mother and her seven-year-old son and four-year-old daughter. The mother was describing how her son was often aggressive toward his little sister and this concerned her greatly. As she was speaking I could observe the children out of the corner of my eye and I saw how the girl was beginning to annoy her brother. She was trying to take the figures he was playing with and he was beginning to get upset, taking them back from her. It struck me that he was on the point of hitting out, so, rather than let this escalate, I went over to him and said, 'It can be hard playing with your little sister, but you're doing a good job, letting her have some of your toys'. He enjoyed the compliment, relaxed and then said, 'Look Tina, you can play with these figures and I'll play with these ones'. In this way, a bout of misbehaviour was avoided, and the child was praised for sharing with his sister. Of course this tactic does not work every time, but it can be very powerful in diverting misbehaviour to notice the good (or slightly good) behaviour that precedes it.

Can children be given too much attention?

Children can certainly be given too much negative attention for troublesome behaviour. Children who are constantly pestering their parents – arguing and whining – have learned that this way of behaving is guaranteed to get a response. Instead, providing attention to children when they are not behaving in this way, for example,

I APPRECIATE YOUR PAYING ME POSITIVE ATTENTION, MUM... BUT IT MAKES IT A BIT DIFFICULT TO WIN AT 'HIDE AND SEEK'...

when they are quiet, pleasant and doing what is asked of them, will, over time, bring about positive changes in their behaviour.

Some parents may be reluctant to praise ordinary behaviour or give a lot of positive attention, fearing it will make their children big-headed or that they might become dependent on the praise they receive. Research shows that children who receive much praise and encouragement – especially for ordinary and simple things – turn out to be the most successful, confident and securely independent adults. When positive attention is genuine and sincere, it is very difficult, perhaps impossible, to provide too much.

Focus on what you want

Catching children being good is essentially about switching your focus to attending to what you want rather than what you don't want. Often parents are very clear about the behaviour they don't want in their children – fighting,

whingeing, staying out late, etc. – but are less clear about
what they do want from them. Instead of your two older
children squabbling and fighting all day, what behaviour
would you like to see? Perhaps you would like to see them
getting along better, or sharing, or playing quietly together. Catching children being good is about thinking
in advance about what you want and going out of your
way to notice this behaviour and make a big deal of it when
it occurs. Remember also to catch yourself being good as a
parent. As I have said earlier it is important to apply these
positive principles to yourself as well as to your children.

Making a shift to consistently focus on what you want,
rather than what you don't want, can make a real difference in your life, transforming your own sense of self,
your relationship with your children and with your
partner.

Tips for going forward

1 Make a note of the specific times your children behave well or better than usual. Be on the lookout to catch them being good.

2 Notice things that happen in your family that you are pleased about and that you would like to see happen again.

Play and special time with children

When I first started to play with my seven-year-old son, it didn't go so well. I realised that I had certain ideas about what we should play together, such as football or the more physical games. When I stepped back and let him lead, I realised he had more of an interest in crafts and making artistic things. This was all new to me, but I let go of my own agenda of how play 'should go' and sat down with my son. I remember how delighted he was when I took an interest in what he was doing. I also learnt so much about him and his talent for crafts and it brought us closer together.

In the last chapter we talked about the importance of parents positively attending to their children, particularly by catching them being good. Now we look at how parents can further promote a positive interaction with their children by setting aside special time to play with them.

Often parents will do everything for their children, except play with them. They will feed and dress them, take them to and from school and ensure they get to bed on time, but in their busy schedule there can be little time left to sit down and play or spend relaxed, fun time with them. Often busy weeks can pass with little quality time spent between parent and child.

There is an idea in society that play between parents and their children is an unimportant activity and a low priority, given all the other things that need to be done. Yet the truth is very far from this. Good play is essential to the well-being and development of children, and play between parent and child is not only rewarding and enjoyable in itself, it also builds a close parent–child relationship which forms the basis for solving discipline problems.

The value of play and special time for children

Play promotes physical, educational, emotional and social development in young children. Through play (aside from having fun) they learn new skills and abilities, express feelings and learn how to get along with other children. It is extremely important for parents to take special time to play with their children for many reasons:

- Playtime can be a relaxing and enjoyable experience for parents as well as for children. In fact, many parents describe these times as among their happiest. Good playtime is a reward in itself to parents, providing an often-missed opportunity to enjoy their child's company away from stress and conflict.

- Playtime brings parent and child closer. Children are more likely to open up to parents before and after playtime. With older children it is often during shared activities that they will reveal concerns or special interests they have. Parents can really get to know their children by spending special time with them.

- Child-centred play allows children to take the lead and make decisions. Children who experience their parents giving them control in play situations are more likely to have a sufficient sense of security to allow their parents to take control in discipline situations. When parents respect children's rules in play, children are more likely in turn to respect parents' rules in other situations.

- Child-centred play is the best way to bring on children's development and to help them learn new things. When adults play with children in a responsive way, they help them learn new language and how to communicate and take turns.

How best to play with children

While there is no one right way to play with children, there are a number of guidelines that can be helpful.

1   Set aside a special time.
Perhaps the most important thing to do is to set aside a special time to play with your children. In a busy parent's schedule, this may need to be

planned in advance and prioritised as something important and not to be missed. Play sessions don't have to be long to be effective. With young children (up to six years of age) short daily play sessions of fifteen minutes can make a real difference. With slightly older children, you might want to have longer times less frequently (two one-hour sessions weekly) based around an activity or hobby.

2   Spend one-on-one time with children.
Special time works best if it only involves one child at a time. While this can put extra demands on parents with many children, there is no replacement for one-on-one time with another person, in terms of getting to know them deeply and building an enduring bond with them. Even if it means slightly shorter or less frequent special times, it is still best to have quality one-on-one times with your children. These are the foundations of good family life.

3   Follow the child's lead.
In good playtime, children should be encouraged to take charge and make most of the decisions. Children have many other arenas in life where parents are

in charge, so playtime is their chance to try out decision-making and to develop confidence. Parents can sit back and follow the child's lead, valuing and affirming their imagination and initiative. With young children this simply means letting the child choose the game or activity and how to play it. With older children it means involving them in the planning of activities and future special time. In both cases it is useful to take time to get to know what your children are interested in and to value and affirm their ideas first. With young children, this can be simply watching carefully what the child is doing and then naming or imitating it. Consider the simple example below.

Two-year-old Sam is playing with blocks. His Dad is sitting down at this level, carefully watching him play. He sees Sam pick up a blue block:

Sam: *Block*

Dad: *Yeah, a _blue_ block.*

Sam puts it on another block.

Dad: *... And you have put it on the _green_ block.*

Sam: *Tower*

Dad (excitement in voice): *You are building a tower ... wow!*

Sam (matching Dad's excitement): *Yeah, a big tower.*

In the above example, the father is not only engaged in enjoyable play with Sam he is also helping him learn language. By naming what Sam is doing, by repeating what he says emphasising key words and by getting down to Sam's level, all this is maximising the connection between them and Sam's rate of learning. It is also critical how the father has slowed down to Sam's pace. While it is easy to rush ahead of your children with new ideas, it is more helpful for them if you slow down and go at their pace. Sometimes simply repeating what they have said or copying their actions is enough to keep the play going and to help your children have the most beneficial experience.

4 Choose interactive, imaginative activities.
The best toys and play materials are those which stimulate a child's imagination and creativity. They don't have to be expensive 'educational' toys. We all see children who turn away from the expensive toy to transform the box and wrapper into an imaginative castle.

The best type of toys are those which allow children to be active and creative rather than passive (as with television viewing) and which allow parent and child to do things together. It is important to have toys that match a child's age and ability level as well as their personality. For older children, choose activities which emphasise cooperation and which allow you to interact with them. For example, going fishing is often a better choice than the cinema as it gives you more of an opportunity to talk and relate together. Below are some suggestions for play and special time to which you can add your own ideas.

Younger children
– play dough, Plasticine

- blocks/Lego (any building or construction kits)
- jigsaws (age level)
- dolls/figures/puppets
- tea set, tool set
- farmhouse, doll's house
- soft toys
- dress up box
- paints, crayons, colours

Older children (6 and upwards)
- jigsaws
- construction kits/models (boats, planes, etc.)
- paints/colours
- creative activities such as making a collage
- board games
- football/outdoor games/special activities (fishing)

Encourage children in play

It's easy to fall into the trap of correcting children when they play. Out of a desire to teach children, parents can find themselves being critical, saying, 'Oh, that doesn't go there', or 'It should be done like this'. I suggest that for special playtime, you go out of your way to encourage children, looking for things they are doing right and showing great interest in their activities. For example, you can use lots of positive comments such as 'I like that colour you have chosen', or 'It was a good idea to turn it around that way', or 'You're really persistent trying to get this house made'. Essentially it is about being a good audience to children in their play, taking a great interest in what they are doing, getting down to their level, providing lots of eye contact and good body language. Using encouraging statements and kind comments helps children continue in their play and promotes a rewarding experience for both parent and child.

Have family special time

As well as individual special time between parent and child, special time for the whole family together is important. Like playtime, this can get lost in the busy weekly

schedule and often needs to be prioritised and planned in advance. Families can set aside a special Sunday meal or family trip at the weekends as a way of spending relaxed, fun time together.

I'd been worried for a long time about my ten-year-old daughter who seemed increasingly unconfident. I realised that I was very distant from her and she was growing up so quickly. So I made time to take up a hobby with her and to help her learn something new. She chose to learn how to play the flute (which was completely new to me). The two of us went to classes together. Funnily enough, she proved to be a better player than me and much of the time she would be helping me out on how to play. Ironically, the fact that she was teaching her Dad rather than the other way round proved to be real boost to her confidence. I learnt I didn't have to 'teach' her anything but just to be with her.

Tips for going forward

1 Set aside a regular special time to play or spend special time with your children individually. For young children, this could be short daily sessions of fifteen to twenty minutes. For older children, this could be less frequently but for a longer period of time, for example in the form of a weekly planned activity.

2 During special time make sure to follow the child's lead, use lots of encouragement and above all have fun.

Encouragement and praise

I realised that I could be down on my children all the time, correcting them every time they did something wrong. Ironically, I was only doing it because I wanted the best for my children, I wanted to make sure they grew up behaving well and knowing right from wrong. But now I know, that while my intentions were good I was on the wrong track. My children need my encouragement and praise much more than my criticism and correction. And this is the best way to teach them how to behave well. It is also the way I enjoy the most!

People often think that the best way to change children's misbehaviour is to criticise and scold them when they misbehave – pointing out the error of their ways, so to speak. However, this approach has a number of drawbacks: excessive criticism can damage a child's confidence and ability to change; it leaves both parent and child upset; and it gives attention to the misbehaviour. It is far more effective for parents to encourage and praise the examples of good behaviour they see. By making this switch in focus you will notice an improvement in your relationship, as it is far more enjoyable and satisfying to encourage rather than criticise.

Often people think that children who are consistently 'bold' or 'naughty' need a lot of criticism and don't deserve praise. The truth of the matter is that these children's confidence is such that they need encouragement far more than other children who are receiving it already. Helping these children see that there are some things that they can do right is the best way to help them get back on the road to improved behaviour and better relationships.

Skills of specific encouragement

When we use encouragement or praise to promote good behaviour in children, we can make sure it gets through to the child by ensuring that it is clear, specific and personal.

ENCOURAGEMENT SHOULD BE CLEAR

You should have the child's full attention before you give encouraging statements. It is less effective to encourage with statements muttered under your breath from another part of the room or when the child is doing something else like watching TV and not really listening. It is important to get down to the child's level, to make eye contact and to use a warm and genuine tone of voice. The child should be in no doubt that he or she is getting a positive message from you. Think of encouragement as the most important message you can possibly give to your children. You really want to make sure it gets through to them.

ENCOURAGEMENT SHOULD BE SPECIFIC

If you want to help children to change positively they need to know exactly which behaviour they are being praised for, and which qualities you are encouraging in them. Vague statements such as 'You are a great boy' or 'Good girl' don't tell a child what you are pleased about, and can soon wear thin and seem insincere. It is more effective to say, 'Thanks for putting out the bins when I asked', or 'It is great to see you sharing with your sister'. These statements help children know exactly what good behaviour you are praising and make it more likely to occur again. It is also important to praise as soon after the desired behaviour as possible so they are in no doubt that it is that behaviour you want to see again.

ENCOURAGEMENT SHOULD BE PERSONAL

The best way to encourage is unique to each parent and child. What is essential though, is that your child experiences your encouragement as personal and genuine. Saying how you feel and expressing this to your child can make a real difference. Often this can be achieved by using an 'I' message. For example: 'I really appreciate the way you cleaned up your room'; or 'Thanks for coming in immediately when I asked you, that means a lot to me'; or 'I really enjoyed playing with you today, I love it when we get on so well.'

It is also very important to be affectionate when encouraging children, especially when they are younger. A simple hug or a pat on the back can speak volumes. Remember, what works in encouragement varies from parent to parent and from child to child. Find out what works for you.

Exceptions/steps in the right direction

Often parents say that they never witness examples of the good behaviour they want in their children. For example, the children never do what they're asked, or they never share with other children. When you are feeling negative and angry it can be hard to notice the positives. However, if you closely observe your children you will notice that there are always times, however short-lived, when they are behaving more positively. If you are serious about helping your children change, it can make a real difference to notice these exceptions. Children need to know there are some things they are doing right, before they can have the confidence to change.

It is important not to wait for perfection or a finished task before you encourage or praise. Change can be gradual and, to ensure that children don't get demotivated, it is important to encourage and praise steps in the right direction. For example, encourage a child when she starts to do her homework: 'I'm pleased to see you sitting down straight away and starting your homework'. You don't have to wait for the homework to be completed. Encouraging the first step of a task helps a child persist and continue to the end.

Double encouragement

The effect of encouragement can be doubled by involving other people. Praising a child in public or in front of important people can make it more powerful and really drive the message home. For example, if Dad has witnessed good behaviour, as well as praising it himself he can double the impact by telling Mum about it in front of the child later in the day. There is often a tendency to nag about misbehaviour, to really go on about what is wrong.

Using encouragement, you can turn this around and really go on about what your child has done right. Tell them repeatedly and everyone else about anything you are pleased about that they have done.

Persist with encouragement

Many children initially reject encouragement and praise. They might shrug it off, saying, 'Of course I didn't do it right', or they may not believe the parent is genuine. If a child has not received much encouragement in the past, it can take a while before he or she can begin to accept the positives you point out. Equally, if encouragement is a new approach for parent and child it can feel awkward at first and, like any skill, it can take a while before it becomes second nature. It is important not to give up if a child initially rejects encouragement. See this as a sign that your child needs the encouragement all the more. Persistence can really pay off.

Think about new ways to get your encouragement through. It might be a case of picking a better time or choosing different things to praise. It might help to change your style of encouragement to ensure it is clear, specific and personal. This all helps the child to experience it as genuine. With older children it can be effective to sit down and talk about what it is you are pleased about and what it is you want from them. You can even explain your new positive approach, saying you want to have a better relationship with them and you believe that positive encouragement is the best way.

I found it hardest to start encouraging my nine-year-old son. I think it was because I had had been critical of him for so long. He was a little suspicious of my intentions at first. He would say 'You are just saying that to me because you want me to do something', or 'Don't try that stuff from the parenting class on me'. Things changed when I sat down with him and explained that I realised that I had been very negative in the past and I wanted to make a change, that I wanted things to be happy between us and wanted to be positive. Slowly he came on board and it began to work. One benefit that surprised me was how he became very encouraging and positive back to me.

Be encouraging towards yourself

You can only truly be encouraging towards your children if you are encouraging towards yourself. In my work I meet many parents who for many reasons find it hard to be positive towards their children. When I listen deeper, I discover that they were never encouraged as children and, in fact, often experienced negative childhoods. In many cases, these parents have taken on board the negative messages from their childhoods and are extremely self-critical, always putting themselves down. Things only change when I can help that parent find a way of being more forgiving, accepting and encouraging of themself. As the mother in the next example states, this change helped both her and her child.

> *With my youngest child, I'm sad to say that I found it really hard to encourage her. I think it was because she was born at a difficult time in my life and things didn't go well from the start. Initially, all I could see was the negatives in her personality and the many behaviour problems I had with her. This was really hard for me as a mother, as I thought I should be having only positive feelings and I used to feel guilty. Change happened when I shared these feelings in a parenting group and realised that I was not alone in having them. As a result I stopped giving myself a hard time for having negative feelings. I was able to forgive myself and let go of my resentment. This freed me up to begin to appreciate the good things my daughter brought into my life. When I stepped back I began to notice lots of things I liked about her presence in my life. I began to understand her more and was more able to be really positive towards her. The encouragement helped us both.*

Tips for going forward

1 Make a list of the behaviours you want to discourage in your children (for example, fighting with one another).

2 Make a list of the behaviours you want to encourage (for example, getting along, sharing, playing well together).

3 Write down how you will specifically encourage any signs, however small, of these positive behaviours.

4 Be encouraging of yourself. Notice the things you like about yourself as a person and a parent.

Using rewards

In the previous steps we have looked at how positive parental attention, using encouragement and play, can be influential in promoting good behaviour in young children and in building a close relationship with them. In this step we look at how rewards and treats can be used to encourage children, and to act as back-up to the praise

IT'S GOOD THAT MY PARENTS BELIEVE IN REWARDING GOOD BEHAVIOUR ... BUT I'M NOT ACTUALLY ALL THAT KEEN ON CARROTS.

and attention you are providing. Rewards can simply be spontaneous treats given when a child is behaving well. For example, 'Thanks for helping with the cleaning up, now I've time to read you a story – which one would you like?', or 'You worked hard on your homework, well done! Would you like an ice-pop from the freezer?'. Rewards can also be planned in advance and given for an agreed behaviour. To illustrate this, let's look at how one mother positively solved a problem she was facing with the help of a reward system.

Using a star chart

Jean had a problem with her six-year-old daughter, Mary, who just wouldn't go to bed on time. Mary would moan and whine at bedtime and think of excuses to delay the process, saying, 'I'm hungry', or 'I need something to drink'. Jean tried many things to get her to go to bed, like cajoling, lecturing, etc., but the more she tried to get her to hurry, the more Mary would dawdle. Even when she got her to her room and into bed, five minutes later Mary would be up again. Jean was exasperated at this and would often lose her patience with Mary.

Talking to her Public Health Nurse, Jean got the idea to use a star chart with Mary to help her go to bed on time. She sat down with Mary to explain about the chart in advance. She explained why Mary needed to go to bed on time and how she had a new star chart to help her do this. She explained that Mary would get a silver star for being in bed by 8 p.m. (that meant that Mary had to start getting ready by 7.30 p.m.) and if she stayed in bed she would get a gold star the next morning. When Mary had five stars she would get an extra treat. Jean asked Mary what she would like as a treat and Mary said an ice-cream. The two of them made up the chart together, divided into the different days, with spaces on each day for two stars. Mary coloured-in the outside of the chart and Jean stuck a picture of Mary asleep on it, to remind her of what the chart was for. They agreed to hang the chart on the bedside wall, where Dad could also see it in the morning.

On the first night, with a little support, Mary got into bed by 8 p.m. Jean praised her, and took out a star and Mary pinned it on the chart. Mary settled down, but ten minutes later she left her room. Jean knew how to handle this: she didn't give out to her or give too much attention, but calmly directed Mary back to her room. In the morning, Mary asked about getting a gold star. Jean explained that she would have to stay in her room for the night to get the gold star. That evening, Mary went to bed on time and got her silver star and a kiss from Mum. She asked about *the gold star and Jean reminded her about staying in the bedroom all night. Sure enough, Mary did this and she got the gold star in the morning. Jean was so pleased about it that she told Mary's father as well.*

As time went on Mary became more used to going to bed on time and staying there until morning. There were still times when she would go to bed late, or come out of her room, but Jean managed these times by firmly insisting that Mary returned to her room, and by ensuring she got little attention when she was out of her room. Jean also made sure not to give the gold star in the morning.

Making rewards effective

The above example illustrates how a reward system can be used as a back-up to encouragement for a younger child. It highlights a number of principles, which make planned rewards effective.

Be clear about the behaviour you want

Often when giving rewards parents are vague about what they want, for example, giving a child a treat for 'being good'. Also, parents often reward the absence of a negative behaviour they don't want, for example, 'not fighting' or 'not staying up late'. The trouble with these approaches is that they don't tell the child exactly what you want; and in the latter example they highlight the behaviour you don't want. For this reason it is important to be very clear and positive about the behaviour you do want and to make sure the child is clear as well. In the above example, Jean rewarded Mary for being in bed at 8 p.m. and for staying in her room until morning, both very clear and positive behaviours.

Use motivating rewards

It is important to use rewards which are of great interest to your child, and which they will work hard for. This varies from child to child and depends very much on your child's age. For younger children, brightly coloured stickers or stars, backed up by small treats, can be enough to motivate them. Older children won't be motivated by stars but will usually be motivated by a points system for good behaviour leading to tangible rewards. For example, you could encourage your nine-year-old son in his studying by giving him a point each evening he does his homework when he comes home from school and before he goes out to play. When he gains an agreed number of points (e.g. five) he can 'cash these in' for a treat, such as choosing a video at the weekend. The trick with children is to make the rewards you normally give them dependent on good behaviour and cooperation. For example, instead of simply giving children pocket money each week, let them earn it through helping out with household chores. When children work hard for something they want, they learn to appreciate it more, and it teaches them about responsibility.

Rewards don't have to be expensive to be effective. Even older children can be motivated by ordinary treats like extra playtime, a special trip, etc. It is important to put some time into thinking which rewards will work for your child. It often helps to ask the child what he or she would like (within limits) as Jean did in the above example.

Examples of good rewards are:

- staying up later
- special time with parents in the evening
- an extra bedtime story
- going shopping with a parent
- a trip out to the park or playground
- taking out a special toy that is not used frequently (e.g. the paddling pool in the garden)
- a trip to McDonalds
- going to the cinema
- choosing a video at the weekend
- having a friend over to tea
- 20 pence extra pocket money

Involve children in the planning

The more children are 'hooked in' and involved in the planning of rewards, the more likely the rewards are to be effective. As seen in the above example, it is a good idea to explain in advance the reward system and the positive reasons for it, making sure the child understands what you want, and answering any questions he or she has. Equally, getting the child involved in making the chart, choosing the stars, etc., all make a difference to the child's motivation. Notice how Jean let Mary colour-in the chart and then let her pin the stars onto it.

Start small

One of the reasons reward systems can sometimes fail is that they may initially be too difficult for the child to

achieve, and when the child fails to get the reward on the first few attempts he or she gives up, feeling disillusioned. For this reason it is important to start small, with behaviour that is easy enough for the child to achieve. For example, with a child who finds it hard to concentrate, instead of only rewarding him for doing his homework for a whole hour, you could reward him with a star for every fifteen minutes he spends concentrating. In the above example, Jean made the task easier for Mary by dividing it into two parts – being in bed at 8 p.m. and staying in her room until morning.

Use lots of encouragement

Rewards aren't a replacement for verbal encouragement and approval. In fact, they work best if they are backed up by lots of positive attention and kind words. Getting others to notice and be involved in reward systems can be very helpful. Notice how Mary's chart was placed on her bedroom wall for her Dad to see and thus add his approval and encouragement.

Rewards work best if they are not used excessively, but only for special occasions or to learn specific behaviours. When a child has learned the desired behaviour the reward system can be phased out over time. For example, when Mary gets into the habit of going to bed on time, Jean can phase out the star system, replacing it with ordinary positive attention. If Mary is still motivated to gain stars, a new desired behaviour can be selected, such as doing her homework at a specified time or coming in when asked.

Tips for going forward

1 Make a list of the rewards that you know will really motivate your children, and which you can easily afford and are happy to give them.

2 Plan with your children a star chart or points system for a specific new behaviour you want to teach them.

Setting rules and helping children keep them

How many rules?

Parents rightly feel obliged to teach their children good social behaviour. While it is important to teach children to think for themselves and to be self-responsible, it is also important to set certain rules and limits and to correct them when they step outside these. You may wonder what is the best way to do this. How can we set rules and limits with children in a way that teaches them self-responsibility? In addition, when we have set a rule, what is the best way to ensure children keep them, or learn from the consequences if they don't? These are the questions we will attempt to answer in this step.

Firstly, encourage children to make as many decisions for themselves as possible. Letting them make many decisions and choices helps them to be independent and to grow up confident and responsible. Many parents create unnecessary rules and lose the opportunity to let children decide about different things. For example, does a parent have to decide what colour socks her five-year-old wears? Does a parent have to decide what toys a child chooses in play? Do the grown-ups always have to decide what the family has for dinner? Of course the decisions children can make and those that a parent must make for them depend very much on their age.

Secondly, give children choices even when you are imposing a limit. For example, you may insist a child does her homework when she comes in from school, but you may give her choices about when and where she does it, provided it is done well. Or you may insist a child eats vegetables with his dinner but let him choose (within reason) which vegetables. Or you may insist a child goes to bed at 8 p.m. but give her choices about the routine prior to going to bed. By giving children options within the limits you set, and by negotiating these with them, you increase their cooperation and self-responsibility.

Thirdly, keep the rules you set with children to a minimum, confining them to those that really matter. One of the errors parents can make is to have too many rules for their children. This is especially true when children are demanding and parents wish to take control. However, too many rules often leads to more conflict, which in turn reduces even further the amount of time children cooperate with their parents' wishes. For this reason it is best to keep rules and commands to a minimum, and focus only on the rules that really matter to you. Once these are chosen, it is important to work hard to ensure that your children comply with them.

Effective commands/assertive commands

People often fall into the trap of issuing commands to children either aggressively or passively, rather than assertively. With aggressive commands, we are more likely to use an angry voice and intimidating body language. However, this can be ineffective, only resulting in the child getting angry in return. Even if the child does what we ask, he or she is likely to be hurt or resentful and less likely to comply in the future.

With passive commands we use a soft whispery voice, hardly gaining the child's attention. In this case the child is likely to ignore what we say or not carry out the request because he or she feels we don't really mean it.

With assertive commands we insist on gaining the child's attention, by getting down to his or her level, gaining eye contact, cutting out distractions, etc. We use a calm, polite and firm voice, while keeping our body language friendly but firm.

Assertive commands are not only the most respectful for both parent and child, they are also by far the most effective way to help children cooperate and do what we say. Learning how to communicate assertively takes a lot of practice, as often we are not aware of what our body language is communicating. Sometimes people communicate with a glaring expression on their face or a trembling in their voice but are unaware of this. Role play is one of the best ways to practice, either in a group, where you can

AND ONE OF THE RULES OF THIS HOUSE IS THAT WE DISCOURAGE AGGRESSION!!

get feedback from other participants, or at home in front
of a mirror, where you can observe yourself. (You might
want to make sure no one else is in the house at the time.)

Use positive commands

As an experiment, I want you to carry out the following
instruction in your imagination. I want you not to think of
a blue kangaroo. Don't think of a blue kangaroo!
    Were you able to carry out this simple instruction? On
average most people find it impossible to carry out a negative command like this because, to understand what is
being asked, you have to visualise a blue kangaroo.
Giving negative or 'don't' commands to children creates
the same problem. If we say 'don't' to a child, for example,
'Don't run in the shop', the child has to visualise himself
running in the shop to understand what we mean. Such a
command immediately focuses him on the behaviour we
don't want and acts almost as a suggestion to carry it out.
In addition, 'don't' commands only tell children what
they can't do (something they often know very well),
and nothing about what they can do. With 'don't' commands we give few ideas to children about how to behave
correctly. Equally, we are more likely to give 'don't' commands angrily, and this sets up the expectation that the
child is about to misbehave. For this reason I suggest you
issue only positive 'do' commands to children. All negatively framed commands can be made positive. All
'don'ts' can be turned into 'dos'. For example:

- 'Don't grab the toys from your sister' can become
  'Please ask your sister to share the toys'.

- 'Don't shout in the house' can become 'Please use a quiet voice in the house'.
- 'Don't hurt your little brother' can become 'Please look after your little brother'.

Make sure your request is clear

When parents ask a child to do something, they often muffle what they say or use vague language. Sometimes they don't even look at the child when they ask something. I remember one parent who used to shout many of her commands to her children from another room. It is best if you make your requests very clear to your children. This means getting down to their level, using a firm but polite tone of voice, ensuring you have their eye contact and making sure they know exactly what you mean. With young children who are preoccupied in something else, this can mean kneeling down beside them, getting their attention and making sure they are looking at you before you tell them what you want.

Give children time to comply

One of the biggest mistakes that parents make is that they don't give children time to comply with a command. They bunch commands together and may have given three or four before the child has had a chance to carry out the first one. This leaves the child confused and burdened and invariably leads to conflict. When you ask a child to do something, I suggest you wait about five seconds before you issue another command or before taking disciplinary action. It can be helpful to count to five silently in your head. This helps to defuse the situation, and gives children time to decide how to comply.

Warnings and reminders are also helpful to children. For example, when children are engrossed in play before bedtime it can be helpful to remind them of bedtime by saying, for example, 'You will have to get ready for bed in ten minutes'. This gives children time to prepare and make choices about how to end their play.

Praise cooperation

It is important to get into the habit of praising children when they cooperate with your wishes. Commenting positively each time they do what you ask takes any 'power victory' out of the experience, and helps children see it as rewarding to be cooperative.

Often parents don't feel like thanking a child when they do something they are told, or they feel it is something the child should do anyway without praise. However, the problem with this approach is that behaviour not rewarded soon disappears. If parents wish to encourage their children's cooperation, thanking them when they do what they are told can make all the difference.

Following through on commands

Even when parents follow all the suggestions above and give their children clear, assertive and positive commands, there will still be times when a child chooses not to comply. It is normal, and indeed healthy, for children to test their parents' rules and limits. Parents must respond to this challenge and ensure children experience the consequences of such testing. This helps them learn to cooperate and understand the effects of their actions.

Logical consequences

We cannot make anyone do what they decide not to. This is especially the case with children. All we can do is offer children a choice between doing what we ask and a consequence for not doing so. The goal is to make it rewarding for them to take the choice we suggest and have an unrewarding consequence when they don't. The more logical these consequences are, the more powerful the lesson is. Examples of good logical consequences are as follows:

- If a child doesn't eat at mealtime, then no food is made available until the next mealtime, even though the child is hungry – the child learns to eat at mealtimes.
- If a child stays off school (possibly feigning illness), then he or she stays in bed for the day – the child learns it is not fun to stay off school.
- If a child comes in one hour late, then he or she has to be in one hour earlier the next evening – the child learns to come in on time.
- If a child has made a mess, then he or she has to clean it up before going out to play – the child learns not to make a mess.
- If a child gets aggressive during playtime, then playtime ends – the child learns to play appropriately.
- If a child dawdles getting ready for bed, then there is no time for a story – the child learns to get ready for bed quickly.
- If a child does not get up by eight in the morning, then he or she has to go to bed an hour earlier – the child learns to get up on time.

Consequences such as those listed above are best offered to children in the form of choices and, if possible, should be thought out in advance, as it can be difficult to think of them in the heat of the moment. Good examples would be, 'You either play with the sand and keep it in the box, or it will be taken away from you – it's your choice' or 'You can either calm down now and play the game, or the game will stop – it's your choice'.

When you do set up a consequence in the form of a choice, you must be prepared to enforce it and follow it

through. The essential thing about enforcing consequences is that it is a time for action and not words. It is
best if a parent follows through calmly and firmly without
reasoning or scolding. Things can be talked about at
another time. Enforcing consequences is a time for action.

*Using choices with my four-year-old daughter
worked like magic for me. She was the type of
child who hated to be told what to do, she hated
anyone ordering her. Giving her choices about what
to do next helped her hold onto some of the control
and retain her dignity. For example, instead of
arguing with her over eating vegetables at dinner,
I'd say 'what vegetable would you like for dinner,
you can have broccoli or carrots'. Or, instead of
getting into a fight at bedtime, I'd say, 'I'll read
you a story when you are sitting in the bed, it is
your choice'. Of course, it meant that I had to plan
ahead and think through potentially conflictual
situations about what choices I could give her, but
it still worked well.*

When–then command

A simple command which gets great results for parents is
the when–then command. This is a positive command
which orders events so that children experience a
natural reward following the completion of a task or
chore. For example, you can say, 'Paul, when you do
your homework, then you can watch TV'. Paul is given
the choice of doing his homework and then having the
reward of watching TV, or the choice of not doing his

homework and having the consequence of not watching TV. Other examples are:

- 'When you do your homework, then you can go out to play.'
- 'When you get ready for bed, then Mummy will read you a story.'

The command can also be rephrased using the words as soon as. For example:

- 'You can have some dessert as soon as you finish your dinner.'
- 'You can watch TV as soon as you get dressed.'

A formula to help children comply with commands

The following step-by-step sequence gives you a formula for issuing effective commands to children and then

IF YOU'RE NAUGHTY I WON'T LET YOU HAVE ANY OF MUM'S FRUITCAKE. IF YOU'RE GOOD YOU WON'T HAVE TO EAT HER COTTAGE PIE EITHER.

helping them to comply by following through with logical consequences:

1 Give the child a clear, positive and assertive command (for example, 'Paul, please turn off the TV now and do your homework').

2 Wait about five seconds for the child to comply.

3 If the child complies, praise him ('Thank you for doing that, Paul').

4 If the child does not comply, give him the choice of a consequence (for example, 'Paul, you can either turn off the TV yourself or I will, which do you prefer?').

5 If the child complies, praise him.

6 If not, enforce consequence (parent goes and turns off the TV).

7 Be sure to ignore protests.

Tips for going forward

1 Make a list of decisions that your children can be encouraged to make for themselves (for example, what games to play, the order of homework subjects).

2 Make a list of the rules that are important for your children to keep (for example, no hitting out, 8 p.m. bedtime).

3 Pick one or two rules which you want to work on next week. Write them down in the form of clear, polite, assertive requests (for example, 'John, please put away your toys', 'Mary, when you finish your homework you can go outside').

4 Pick a logical consequence to each of these requests, should your child choose not to comply. You may be able to think of more than one.

5 Follow the step-by-step formula to help enforce the requests you make.

Ignoring misbehaviour

In the first four steps we showed how important parents' attention is to their children. We talked about how you can provide your child with lots of positive approving attention, through play, encouragement and rewards.

In Step 6 we look at the opposite technique – stopping negative behaviour by reducing the attention it receives. We need to remember that even negative attention such as nagging, criticising or shouting all give some attention to the misbehaviour and make it likely to continue. Behaviours such as tantrums, whingeing and minor squabbles depend on the attention of an audience and can be eliminated if they are actively ignored.

What is ignoring?

Ignoring misbehaviour is about paying it as little attention as possible. It is about not getting drawn into rows or screaming matches, but instead remaining calm and not taking the 'bait' of children's misbehaviour. It could be sitting out a young child's tantrum, not responding to a child's nagging, calmly getting on with a job despite a child's whining or calmly walking away from an older child's excessive protests. It is also about not taking misbehaviour personally and not dwelling on it. While a child's misbehaviour can be very upsetting, good ignoring is about not letting it get to you, or not holding on to it, but moving on from it quickly to find examples of good behaviour you want.

Ignoring is definitely not easy. In fact it may be the hardest idea introduced in this book. Many parents think they are ignoring a behaviour but are inadvertently giving it attention via their body language, for example by looking stern or disapproving, or by the fact that they are getting annoyed or emotional. While the child is receiving this type of unconscious attention, the behaviour will still continue. Equally, the silent treatment, or not talking to someone for the day, is not active ignoring.

Indeed, such strategies can be counterproductive, building up resentment in both parent and child.

Ignoring is not an alternative to positive approving attention

Ignoring is only effective when there are other times during which children receive warm approving attention from their parents. For this reason I emphasise the first four steps at this point in the book, which are about providing positive attention to children and forming good and enjoyable relationships with them. These positive experiences are like investments in the 'bank', to be used at times of conflict or misbehaviour. When children see their parents' attention as valuable or when there are many positive times between parents and children, they are more likely to work to seek parental approval. Children are more likely to give up negative behaviours when parental attention is withdrawn.

In addition, there are many situations when it is inappropriate to ignore a child. For example, if your son is crying because he has been hurt or is worried about something, then maybe what he needs is to be soothed and comforted by you, or for you to listen carefully to what has happened, acknowledging his feelings (see Step 8). The critical test is to reflect on whether your attention is making the situation worse or better. Is the attention you are providing increasing or decreasing your child's upset or crying? For example, if your child is sulking because he can't have a toy and you talk to him about it, only to find him more angry, trying to argue about getting the toy, then maybe it is a good decision not to attend to him and give him more space. You can talk to him later when there is a better chance of a more constructive conversation, or of distracting him with a new activity. Ignoring is essentially about you being in charge of your own responses. It is about being able to choose not to respond negatively and being able to choose how and when you respond positively to your child.

How to make ignoring work

Target specific behaviours

Active ignoring works best if it is used to target specific behaviours. Parents should plan in advance which behaviours they want to reduce and whether they can ignore these. Remember, it is up to parents to decide which behaviours they can ignore and this can vary from family to family. For example, some parents can ignore their children's swearing, but others feel this needs to be dealt with by another sanction (for example, 'Time Out' – see the next chapter). The types of behaviours with which ignoring can work very effectively are:

- whingeing
- temper tantrums
- smart talk
- cheek
- protests
- messy eating
- pulling faces
- minor squabbles
- swearing

Ignore thoroughly

Active ignoring involves giving no attention whatsoever to the child's behaviour. This means turning the body completely away and making no eye contact. It is also important to have a calm, relaxed expression on your face. If you communicate that you are angry or upset through your body language, the child may feel that he has 'got to you' and that you are likely to give in if he persists.

Ignore consistently

Active ignoring is not easy, especially when it is first applied. Children may have learned that the best way to get their parents to do what they want is by whingeing and kicking up a fuss. When the parent responds differently by not giving in, the child may intensify the whingeing and shouting to get them to change their mind, before giving up and trying something else. In a nutshell, the behaviour may get worse before it gets better. If you decide to use active ignoring as a tactic you must be prepared to apply it consistently each time the target behaviour occurs and to follow it through on each occasion.

Return positive attention as soon as possible

When a child does give up the negative behaviour, for example, when she gives up protesting or the tantrum stops, it is important to return positive attention, perhaps with a distraction or the suggestion of some positive activity. This is often not easy as the parent may be angry and upset after a period of misbehaviour and may use the opportunity now that the child is 'quiet' to scold or criticise her. However, this can restart the misbehaviour and stop the child learning the value of good positive behaviour. Active ignoring only really works when it is completed with a return to positive attention. For example, if your three-year-old daughter goes into a tantrum because she wasn't allowed play with an inappropriate toy (e.g. sharp scissors), when you notice her coming out of the tantrum, rather than lecturing her about the original behaviour and thereby running the risk of reopening the argument, this is a good time to suggest a new activity in an upbeat, positive manner. You could say, for example, 'Oh now you can play with the Lego or the crayons', or 'I think it might be time to make some tea, would you like to help?'. The point is that you are looking for a way to move on quickly from the original problem and to help your child get back on track with positive behaviour.

As you become more thorough in your ignoring, the period of misbehaviour will become quite short as the child learns that nothing can be gained by persisting and begins to change her behaviour to seek the benefits of your positive attention.

Continue to encourage positive behaviour

If you do decide to ignore a certain behaviour, you can double the impact of this by targeting the opposite positive behaviour with specific encouragement. For example, if you are going to ignore minor squabbles when they occur between your children, it is important to praise them any time you see them getting along better, or sharing with each other.

With younger children it can be helpful to give them distractions and specific suggestions of other positive behaviours instead of the misbehaviour, for example, 'No, you may not turn on the television, but you may play with your Lego', or 'Why don't you do some drawing instead?'.

Ignoring my son's complaining and whining about his dinner was one of the hardest things I learnt to do. I think it was that I took it all personally. If he was saying horrible things about the food, it would really bother me. I'd try to ignore him for a bit and then I would give in and then argue and cajole him. I realised that the fact that I finally caved in and gave attention was making things a lot worse. Things changed when I was able not to let things get to me. For example, instead of arguing when he complained about the food, I would simply say in a matter-of-fact way, 'You don't have to eat it if you don't want to, but there won't be any more food until next meal time', and then get on and eat my own dinner and chat with the rest of the family who were enjoying the meal. When I stopped arguing his complaining stopped. He still tested me later asking for a snack before the next meal and I'd respond, 'Oh no snacks now, but we will all be having dinner at six'. He would then complain and argue, but I simply remained calm and got on with something else. At the next dinner he did eat his meal. I must say I was tempted to gloat, 'Now don't you see that I'm not trying to poison you, it is good food', but I bit my tongue, and ensured I was positive, telling him I was delighted to see him trying his food. This new approach really worked, though it was hard in practice.

Remain calm

Perhaps the most difficult aspect of effective ignoring is remaining calm. It is no surprise that stress management or relaxation techniques are among the biggest selling topics in books within the health field. In most bookshops you will find dozens of books which detail excellent ideas on remaining calm and controlling stress. Below are some of the main ways people remain calm in difficult situations and I suggest you seek further information as you need it.

Think differently

When people are angry or upset they are usually thinking in a negative way about the situation they are in. For example, when confronted by your child's misbehaviour you might think, 'He's doing this on purpose', or 'This will never change'. Such thoughts are likely to make you more angry and helpless. However, if you can think differently during these situations, this can really help you cope better. Imagine if, instead of thinking the above, you say to yourself, 'This is a bad day for her, she's probably tired, she'll be better tomorrow', or 'She's testing the limits today, the best way for me to help her change is to firmly and calmly respond'. Such positive thoughts will have the effect of making you feel calmer and more capable of dealing with the situation.

Talk things through

Talking through how you feel with a partner or friend away from the conflict can be very helpful. Telling someone how negative you feel at times can make these feelings more manageable and less overwhelming. In this way it is very important to create supportive relationships in your life, where you can 'let off steam' if you need to.

Practice relaxation

Learning to relax is something which gets easier with practice. When people take time out each day to relax they can more easily draw on this resource in conflict. There are many different ways to relax such as:

- deep breathing exercises or meditation
- muscular relaxation or special exercises (for example, yoga)
- positive visualisation (for example, recalling in your mind beautiful and relaxing scenes, from a holiday perhaps, or a favourite lake walk)
- doing something you really enjoy such as reading or walking, or even doing the garden

The trick with relaxation is to make it a daily habit. The more you know what it feels like to be relaxed and the more you practise being relaxed, the more easily you will be able to switch into that mode in a stressful situation. Remember, you feel nearly as relaxed recalling a peaceful time as you did during that peaceful time.

Tips for going forward

1 Target one or two behaviours which you can actively ignore next week to eliminate them (for example, whingeing and protesting).

2 Identify the positive opposite behaviours and plan to encourage, praise and reward them each time they occur (when your child does what he is asked quietly and without protest).

3 Take time out to relax next week.

4 Visualise yourself calmly responding to a discipline problem, and not giving attention to the misbehaviour.

Time Out and other sanctions

For difficult behaviours which cannot be ignored, and for children who consistently do not do what their parents tell them, a technique called Time Out can be very useful in helping parents manage. Time Out is basically a way of interrupting difficult behaviour, and breaking from an interaction that is negative and damaging. It teaches children how to separate from a situation and how to calm down. It gives parents a means of discipline which allows them to feel in control, which respects the child and which is a much more realistic, effective and acceptable alternative than slapping.

Time Out is a formalised version of what parents have being doing for years when confronted with their children's misbehaviour – sending them to their room to calm down or asking them to stand in the corner or outside the door. In this section I suggest a formula for Time Out which can make it effective in most circumstances.

Explain Time Out in advance

It is important to sit down with children in advance to explain to them about Time Out. It is important to be positive about the purpose, for example, you might explain that it is about helping them to get on better together, or learning better ways of resolving disagreements other than hitting out. Explain that it is about helping everyone – children and parents – to calm down in angry situations, and avoid rows and shouting which might otherwise occur. There are a number of key points that need to be covered in the explanation:

Which behaviour?

Children need to be absolutely clear which behaviour will lead to Time Out (for example, hitting out, or breaking things). Parents should stick to this and not include other behaviours in the heat of the moment.

Where?

Children should know where Time Out will take place. This ideally should be a safe place where there are not too many distractions. A hallway or bedroom is often used. For younger children, a chair facing the corner can be sufficient, though it may be necessary to have a back-up room if the child refuses to stay in the chair. The Time Out place should not be a scary or unsafe place such as a shed or a bathroom where medicines are kept. If you feel the child is likely to be distressed by going to Time Out you may wish to show him exactly where he will have to go in advance, reassuring him that it is simply a way of helping him to behave better.

How long?

Research shows that Time Out only needs to be short (about five minutes) to be effective. It should not be longer than ten minutes unless the child continues to make a fuss. The essential rule is that children need to be quiet for at least two minutes before they can come out. This means that if they protest, shout or scream, they will have to stay there longer. The goal of Time Out is to interrupt negative behaviour and to help children learn self-control and how to calm down. If they are let out while they are protesting or still angry, this defeats the purpose.

A formula for implementing Time Out

1 Misbehaviour occurs.

2 Parent gives warning, if appropriate – 'If you throw another toy you will have to go to Time Out'. (For some behaviours, for example, hitting, a warning may not be appropriate and the child should immediately go to Time Out.)

3 Misbehaviour occurs again, so parent insists child goes to Time Out.

4 (A) For a younger child (under five or up to six): The child can be guided to the Time Out chair by the parent taking his hand. The parent should do this calmly and firmly, avoiding getting drawn into an argument. If the child does not settle and keeps leaving the Time Out chair, he can be placed in a back-up place (such as the hallway).

(B) For an older child (over six): The parent adds on minutes to the Time Out period to a maximum of ten minutes (e.g., 'If you don't go now to Time Out you will have to spend longer there' or 'That is six minutes for arguing'). If the child continues to refuse, the parent offers a choice between Time Out and a back-up sanction – 'Right you either choose to go to Time Out for ten minutes of you miss X (e.g., a favourite TV programme) ... it's your choice'. If the child refuses to go at this point the sanction is enforced and Time Out is dropped

A formula for ending Time Out

1 The parent ensures the child stays in Time Out for the selected period or until the child has been quiet for at least two minutes. It is important that the parent does not give in to the child's protests or screams, otherwise he will learn that the way to get out of Time Out is by protesting.

2 If the child refuses to come out of Time Out at the end of the time period, the parent simply ignores this and makes no comment.

3 When the child comes out of Time Out the parent does not criticise or nag about the misbehaviour, but

is pleasant, offering the child a suggestion of new positive behaviour (for example, 'Do you want to go and play now?'). The misbehaviour has now been dealt with.

Time Out is about choices

Note how in the above flow chart the child has many choices. He can choose to give up the misbehaviour when he is warned, or he can choose either to go to Time Out or not to go and then incur a sanction. Time Out works best when children's choices and thus their responsibility are emphasised. This makes Time Out likely to be more cooperative and more effective in teaching children how to take responsibility for their own actions.

Using back-up sanctions to make Time Out effective

Time Out is essentially about giving a child a choice. The crucial thing is to help the child choose voluntarily to go there. This helps the child learn self-control and take responsibility. If a child refuses to go to Time Out, having a back-up sanction can be very effective. For example, the parent can offer the child a choice, 'You either choose to go to Time Out or you miss your favourite TV programme'. It is crucial that parents think ahead about the type of sanctions they might use, so that in any discipline situation they will have a range of options open to them. Sanctions are best if:

1 They are short.
Research shows that sanctions can work just as well if they are short. Being grounded for one afternoon can be enough to ensure the child has learned his lesson. If sanctions go on too long, for example being grounded for a month, they can become unen-forceable and cause resentment in the child. Another advantage of short sanctions is that the child can get back on track and have new opportunities to behave well as soon as possible.

2 They affect mainly the child.
It is pointless for parents to choose a sanction which penalises themselves as much or even more than the child, for example when a parent has to miss the football match he also wanted to go to. It is best to choose a sanction which involves the child and not the parent experiencing the loss.

DAD! MUM SAYS
YOU'VE LET THIS
TIME OUT
PERIOD GO ON
WAY
TOO
LONG!

3   They are within the control of the parent.
It is best if the parent can easily enforce the sanction. For example, ensuring the child does extra chores may be difficult for some families and it may be better to opt for something else, such as loss of pocket money. The choice of sanctions is individual to each family and child.

4   They are logically related to the misbehaviour.
For example, if a child has hit a friend, it is logical that the child is not allowed to visit that friend for tea. Other examples of possible sanctions are:

- not being allowed to watch TV for one evening
- not being allowed use the bike for one afternoon
- being grounded for a day
- missing a favourite TV programme
- no playtime
- cancelling a trip
- losing pocket money
- earlier bedtime
- not being able to choose a video

Time Out for parents

Time Out is essentially about interrupting an escalating row or a negative way of communicating. Often in discipline situations parents can get so frustrated that they lose their own tempers or become very upset. At these times it is likely that you will say or do something you regret. It is important for parents to find ways of stopping this escalating – nipping this anger 'in the bud'. Time Out used for parents themselves is a good way of achieving this – when you feel yourself getting too angry or upset to deal with a situation you can choose to withdraw from the child in order to calm down. You can then return to the situation when you are in a better frame of mind.

Time Out is not for everyone!

Time Out is a technique that can be hard to apply and isn't for everyone. Many parents choose not to use it or only keep it in reserve for difficult situations. In addition, it is not a replacement for the positive preventative aspects of parenting. Time Out provides a way of managing difficult situations and getting through difficult times with children in a manner that is least damaging and destructive. I believe it is a far better alternative to slapping, shouting and other negative responses. In itself, however, it does not teach a child how to positively behave and only works when you are providing your children with lots of praise, encouragement and positive attention in other contexts that provide this positive guidance. In the next Step, we look at the area of talking problems through with children, helping then think through how to positively behave. This important step brings all the other ones together.

We found Time Out hard to implement in our house with our six-year-old son. Often the Time Out itself would end up as a battle of wills and was becoming counter-productive. When we reflected about it we realised that we were making a number of mistakes. First, we hadn't really talked the idea through with our son to explain it to him and to gain his cooperation. Second, we were implementing it in a bit of an authoritarian manner and were probably arguing too much with him as we sent him to Time Out, rather than saying little, being calm, persistent and firm. To remedy this, we sat down away from the problem and talked the reason for Time Out through with him. By listening to him we realised that he disliked the fights as much as we did, but also that he felt that we were doing as much of the shouting as he was (this challenged us to reflect carefully about our own behaviour). We then explained a more positive reason for Time Out, that it was literally a time for both of us to take a break from a situation and to calm down. We explained that it wasn't because we didn't love him or that he was a bad child, but that we really did love him and just wanted to find ways for everyone to get on better. In addition, we decided to emphasise his choices (about giving up the misbehaviour when warned, or about choosing to go to Time Out or getting a sanction). We weren't going to 'force him any more'.

This talking it through with him, really helped make Time Out more cooperative. It could still be difficult to implement, but we realised that much of the challenge was in controlling our own responses ensuring they were calm and respectful.

Tips for going forward

1 Identify a behaviour for which you could use Time Out. Plan it carefully, deciding when, where and how.

2 Make a list of sanctions which you can use as back-up for Time Out.

3 Follow the step-by-step formula as a way of making Time Out effective.

4 Use Time Out for yourself if you feel you are becoming too angry in a discipline situation.

Talking things through/
Family meetings

> *Family meetings made a huge difference to our family life. Organising a regular time when we could all be together, to talk things through, to plan things and just to have fun together really transformed things. We became much closer as a result and even when my children became teenagers they still made a commitment to be around on a family night.*

Just as in this book we have encouraged you to 'press the pause button' so you can reflect about your own feelings and actions, so it is also important to help your children to learn to pause and reflect also. The most effective long-term way to help children behave well and be responsible as they grow up is to help them express and understand their feelings and to think through the consequences of their actions. You want to help them learn how to respect-fully communicate and to discover solutions to problems that take into account their own feeling and needs as well as those of others. The best way to do this is to make sure you have plenty of time to talk and particularly to listen to your children, both when things are going well and when problems arise.

The 'techniques' described so far in this book to manage behaviour problems, such as Time Out, Ignoring and Sanctions, only work in the long term when children have time to reflect on their actions and to discover new ways of behaving. This helps children to understand their own feelings and those of other people, to think through the consequences of their actions and to discover positive alternatives to misbehaviour which are good for them and other people. Often a good way to do this is to set aside time to talk to your children both on a one-to-one basis and also as a family together during family meetings.

Talking problems through

Often parents make the mistake of trying to talk a problem through with a child at a time of conflict. As discussed in previous sections, what is called for at these times is withdrawing attention from the misbehaviour, helping children learn by experiencing consequences to their actions, and maybe a cooling-off period for both parent and child. Generally, it is better to talk problems through with children away from the conflict situation at a differ-ent time when everyone has calmed down. It is a good idea to set up a particular time where you can sit down with the child when you both won't be distracted and which doesn't conflict with anything else (don't select a time during your child's favourite TV programme). In addi-tion, try and allow a bit of time for problem-solving sessions, as talking things through with children can take time. Rushing can prevent either parent or child from being heard and may lead to conflict.

Talking things through can be divided into different stages: Listening, Speaking up, Thinking up solutions, Choosing the best solution, Follow-up. These different stages of problem solving are covered in much more detail in Steps 5 to 8 in Part 2 of the book dealing with teenagers. I advise you to read these in conjunction with the present shorter chapter, particularly if you are interested in how you can use these ideas to reduce conflict and solve serious problems.

1. Active listening

Listening is probably the most important communication skill of all. When we truly listen, we step out of our own shoes into those of another person. We try to understand the world as they see it, not just as we see it. Such listening is a great service to another person as we all need to be understood. Being understood by another person helps us to understand ourselves. Active listening is very important to children. As well as being the best form of positive attention, it helps them understand their thoughts and feelings and those of other people, as well as bringing parent and child closer together.

Yet listening is also probably the most difficult skill of all. Most of us have no training in it and it requires a lot of effort on the part of the listener, especially when there is conflict between the listener and the person being listened to. Children in particular are often not listened to. Their thoughts, feelings and viewpoints generally aren't seen as being as important as those of adults. Instead of listening, parents often fall into the trap of giving advice, criticising, or coaching – all useful skills at times but not when we are actively listening to understand a child's feelings. Consider the following responses to a child:

> **Paul** (upset): *James grabbed the computer game from me.*

> **Parent:** *Well, you shouldn't have been playing with it so long (criticism); or*
> *Why don't you play with something else? (advice); or*
> *Oh, don't worry, it's not so bad (coaching); or*
> *Let me go and talk to James (rescuing).*

Active listening involves giving children your full attention. It involves setting aside anything else you are doing to really concentrate on what they are saying (verbally and non-verbally). Perhaps the two most important aspects of listening are: (a) reflecting back to children what they are saying so they feel understood and (b) acknowledging their feelings. Consider now some alternative listening responses:

> **Paul** (upset): *James grabbed the computer game from me.*

> **Parent:** *Sounds like you are upset. Sit down and tell me what happened (sensing the child's feelings and encouraging the child to say more); or*
> *Poor you, I know how much you like playing that game (acknowledging the child's feelings).*

In the above examples, the parent is validating the child's feelings and attempting to see the problem from his point of view. Sometimes simply repeating what the child has said, or nodding encouragingly, can be sufficient to help the child feel listened to and encouraged to express more.

Sometimes listening and gaining a new understanding of how your child is feeling is sufficient to help solve a problem. Consider the example below:

> *My six-year-old son used to be always acting the clown in front of other children and adults. It used to really bother me, because I thought he looked stupid and that people were laughing at him rather than with him. I used to feel embarrassed and would snap at him. I remember one time when he was upset, I sat down and listened to him, he blurted out that he felt he could do nothing right, that everyone thought he was a fool. I suddenly realised that the reason he probably 'acted the clown' was to get the approval he desperately craved. More difficult to realise was the fact that I was part of the problem, by being critical and embarrassed by him. I resolved to get to know him differently, to believe in him as my son and to defend him against other people's criticisms.*

2. Speaking up assertively

As well as listening, it is important that, as a parent, you are able to give your own point of view, especially when you feel strongly about something or when it is an important discipline issue. But it matters a lot how you do this. Often people fall into the trap of blaming, or not acknowledging their own feelings. Good communicators acknowledge their feelings, express their positive intentions, and focus on what they want. This is not only the most assertive and respectful way of communicating, it is also the most effective and the most likely way you will get your child to listen. Consider the following examples of ineffective versus effective 'speaking up':

Ineffective: *You never do what you are told. You are really bold (over-negative, over-general, blaming)*.

Effective: *Look, I want you to put the toys away now, as we are going to have dinner (clear request with a positive intention)*.

Ineffective: *You are such an inconsiderate child, you always make me late (excessive blaming, damaging 'you' message)*.

Effective: *I feel frustrated when you don't get up on time for school. You see, it makes me late for work and I need to get to work on time. I would like it to go a lot smoother in the mornings (clear 'I' message, parent focuses on what he or she wants from the child)*.

3. Thinking up solutions

Once you have understood your child's point of view and expressed your own feelings, you are now in a position to think with your child of alternative solutions to the problems you are both facing. Rather than simply giving your own solutions it is important to hold back and encourage the child to come up with solutions himself. This can be done by asking questions such as: 'How do you think you can solve this?', 'How can you ensure you get home on

SO WHAT I'M SAYING IS I'D LIKE YOU TO BE QUIET WHEN I'M WATCHING THE TV NEWS. NOW FOR THE MAIN POINTS OF MY ARGUMENT AGAIN...

time?', 'What other ways can you get a go on the computer without hitting out?'. Though it may be tempting to come up with your own answers, it is crucial to proceed at the child's pace and to wait for him to generate the solutions. Children are far more likely to carry through solutions they have generated themselves. You will be surprised at how even young children, when given time, can come up with solutions which are as good as or even better than those thought up by parents.

It is important to help children generate as many alternative solutions as possible. Try not to be critical at this stage; encourage your child's creativity and listen to all the ideas he comes up with. These can include solutions tried successfully in the past. For example, your son may remember that when he stayed away from certain boys in the class on previous occasions he didn't get into trouble. Once talked about and understood, these past solutions are more easily repeated.

I was surprised at how a problem-solving approach worked with my four-year-old son as I thought he was too young to think constructively. He used to get into big fights with his little two-year-old brother, Sam, over sharing and I used to jump in and 'solve the problem for them' and this would lead to tears. After pausing to think about it I decided to handle things differently. Instead of jumping in, I backed off and simply asked him questions like, 'Oh we have got only one helicopter and two boys wanting to play with it, what can we do?', or 'What can you give Sam to play with, while you play with the helicopter?' Surprisingly he would often come up with good solutions such as, 'We can take turns', or 'He can have the crayons while I'm playing'.

4. Choosing the best solution

Now it is time to help the child decide which solutions he is going to use. During this stage the emphasis is on helping children think through the consequences of the ideas suggested in the last stage, in order to identify those which will have the best results, both for them and for other people. Frequently, children come up with unrealistic or inappropriate solutions. However, rather than criticising, you can guide them by asking them to think of the consequences. For example, as a way of getting to use his brother's computer, a child might suggest taking a turn without asking. But on thinking it through he realises that this could get him into more trouble if his brother finds out and refuses to let him use the computer at all.

5. Follow-up

When the best solution(s) is chosen, it is important to arrange a time to talk again to review how the child is getting on. Often things aren't solved immediately and you need to be there to support and encourage them.

To give an example of these five stages in action, consider the following scene of a father sitting down to talk to his nine-year-old son, who hit another boy at school.

(1) ACTIVE LISTENING

Father: *You know I said earlier I wanted to talk to you about what happened in school.*

John: *It wasn't my fault, Robert started it* (whining defensively).

Father (calmly): *What happened exactly?* (father does not get into a quarrel but listens to the child to hear his perspective).

John: *Well, we were out in the yard, playing football. Robert started teasing me, so I hit him.*

Father: *It wasn't very nice of him to call you names.*

John: *No.*

Father: *You must have been angry* (father picks up on his son's feelings and helps him feel understood).

John: *Yes* (nods), *and then I got into trouble ... Mrs O'Reilly sent me to the line.*

Father: *Sounds like you feel it was unfair, that*

you think Robert should have got into trouble as well (acknowledges feelings).

John: *Yeah.*

(2) SPEAKING UP

Father: *Do you know why Mrs O'Reilly sent you to the line?* (father helps child think through the consequences of his actions).

John: *Because I hit him?*

Father: *Yeah, while I'm sorry you were called names in school, we have to find other ways of solving it than hitting out. I don't like when you get into trouble in school, because I want you to get on well and be happy there* (father expresses his feelings for his son, his positive intentions and what he wants to happen).

(3) GENERATING SOLUTIONS

Father: *Can you think of a way to handle it without hitting him?*

John (thinks): *I don't know.*

Father: *Come on, you're often very good at school, I am sure you can think of something* (father points out that there are times his son behaves well in school, thus encouraging him to think of solutions).

John (thinking): *I suppose I could tell him to stop.*

Father: *Exactly ... a perfect way ... can you think of anything else?*

John: *I could just walk away.*

Father: *You could just walk away ... anything else?* (father is encouraging and positive about each of the solutions his child generates; he doesn't put them down or criticise).

John: *I could tell the teacher ... but she never really listens to me.*

Father: *I could have a word with her then?*

John (thinks): *I don't know.*

Father: *You're not sure about that. Maybe you want to think about that one* (father lets child decide, thereby helping him to take responsibility).

John: *Yeah.*

(4) CHOOSING THE BEST SOLUTION

Father: *Let's look at what ideas you've got. If Robert jeers at you again, you can just walk away, or you can tell him to stop ... or you can have a word with your teacher, or I could step in and have a word with her?* (father summarises the solutions and helps child make a plan). *What one do you think is best?*

John: *I'll just walk away when he jeers me.*

Father: *That sound like a good choice.*

(5) FOLLOW-UP

Father: *We will talk again tomorrow to see how you get on* (father sets a time to review the plan).

John: *OK, Dad.*

Family meetings

Family meetings are an excellent way of solving family problems and preventing them from arising in the first place. By having a regular time to meet, you ensure there is always a time in the busy week where you can sit down to spend time with your children to discuss any important issues. They give you an opportunity to stay connected with your children and keep the lines of communication open. They can be used to talk together about important issues, have fun, make plans (such as for holidays), negotiate family rules (such as how much TV to watch, or who does the washing up), etc. Though they can be difficult to initially establish, family meetings can have a transforming effect. Many parents describe them as invaluable in completely altering the tone of family life from one of conflict and distance to one of cooperation and closeness. In addition, it is a good idea to establish the routine of family meetings when your children are younger, when they are much more likely to be open to them. It becomes a little more tricky to start family meetings with teenagers. (In Part 2, Step 8, we will consider how to involve teenagers.)

Tips on running family meetings

1 Meetings work best if they are in the context of a 'family night' which involves other activities such as a family meal or a family game or another fun activity.

2 Prepare for the meeting and make sure there is an agenda. As well as deciding what you want to raise as the parent, find out what your children want to discuss. The more you can make the meetings relevant to their concerns the more involved they will be. A good way to prepare is to have a notice board in the kitchen to which children can pin things they want to discuss.

3 Meetings run best when they are run democratically, with a special emphasis on trying to reach consensus or 'win–win' agreements. Though parents might initially lead, it can help to alternate the role of chair and give someone else the task of writing down decisions, and another person the responsibility of keeping track of time.

4 Make sure everyone gets a chance to speak (even the very youngest) and a fair share of the time. The most important role you have as the parent is being a listener.

5 Use the problem-solving steps above: listening, speaking up, thinking up solutions, choosing the best solutions, etc.

6 Don't be in any rush to solve things immediately. It can take a couple of meetings to solve problems and often the most important thing is to hear and appreciate everyone's point of view. Write down any decisions and plans that are made and make sure to have a follow-up meeting to review how everyone is getting on.

In running our family meetings, the children would often bring up things that I didn't think were that important, but in hindsight I realise how important they were to them. On one occasion, my daughter put on the agenda how she didn't like her brother calling her names. When I listened, I was surprised at how hurt she was by this and it was great to see her articulating her feelings. Her brother, to his credit was able to listen and also listed his own complaints, but the end they reached an understanding. Though I wasn't involved directly in this problem, solving it in the family meeting brought us all closer together.

Tips for going forward

1 When having a problem with one of your children, set aside some one-on-one time to talk it through with them. Remember to listen first, to speak up assertively and to encourage your child to come up with some solutions.

2 Think about establishing a family night in your family. Maybe talk to your children individually about it and then call a family meeting to discuss the idea.

PART 2

BEING A PARENT OF A TEENAGER

Pausing to understand teenagers

He just doesn't listen any more and is so secretive and moody. He thinks that we [his parents] *are for the birds and just wants to be with his friends all the time.*

She's become so argumentative and abusive. Anytime we ask her to do anything she starts World War Three in the house.

Becoming a parent of a teenager can be a troubled and stormy time. The young open child who chatted happily to you can suddenly become this argumentative and resentful teenager who challenges everything you say. Teenagers can become secretive and suspicious and you can feel redundant and locked out of their lives. In addition, you can be full of fears for your teenager. There are so many pressures on teenagers to be involved in drugs and alcohol or to become sexually active at too young an age. With their increasing independence, you can also fear

for their safety, worrying that they might be attacked or placed in very unsafe situations. You struggle with setting boundaries and limits with a teenager who can resent your authority as a parent. Michael and Terri Quinn* describe how the crisis of children becoming teenagers can hit parents at a difficult time. Parents are usually in their forties or fifties at the time and may be going through their own midlife crisis. At this stage of life parents are often wondering about the direction of their own lives and careers, sometimes feeling that life has passed them by. Having teenagers who seem to have endless opportunities and who appear ungrateful can stir up a lot of emotion in parents, even causing them to feel envious. Alternatively, parents may be looking forward to a quieter period in their life, only for this to be rudely disturbed by the arrival of a noisy and demanding teenager. In this context, it is understandable for parents to react negatively to this stormy period, to lose sight of the bigger picture and miss out on the enjoyable aspects of parenting a teenager.

---

* See Quinn and Quinn (1988), listed in 'Further Reading' at the back of the book.

It's difficult for teenagers too

The transition from child to adult is difficult for teenagers also. So many changes occur in these short years that it is not surprising that they feel at times confused, frightened and lacking in confidence. Physically, their bodies grow and change in ways that might make them feel awkward and self-conscious. Emotionally, they can be subject to great mood swings as they discover the range of human emotions. From intense feelings of love and infatuation to anger and hatred, teenage emotional life can be like a roller coaster. Physically, teenagers become fully developed and can experience intense sexual feelings that can be alarming to them, especially if they have no one to talk to about what is going on. Intellectually, teenagers also make great gains, being able to analyse things and to develop their own opinions and views. They can begin to see the inadequacies in the parental world (and often are very eloquent in pointing this out) and wonder about their role and meaning in life.

Teenagers are under pressures, some of which are greater than in previous years, and need the support of their parents more than ever.

Navigating the teenage storm

When facing the crisis of the teenage years, many parents react by trying to take control. They may become authoritarian and strict, battling with their teenagers to ensure they toe the line. Alternatively, other parents avoid their teenagers' problems and back down from every conflict, effectively giving up at trying to influence their teenagers or to be involved in their lives. Both these approaches are problematic: the young person with authoritarian parents may rebel even more strongly, escalating the conflict, or they may go 'underground' with their problems, hiding more things from their parents. The teenager with permissive parents may feel uncared for and neglected and, without parental supervision, get involved in out-of-control and unsafe behaviours. Both approaches rob teenagers of having involved parents who can support them through the difficulties they face.

As discussed earlier, this book aims to describe a 'middle way' approach to parenting that shows how you can stay supportively involved in your teenagers' lives, while also being firm, to ensure that they learn to take responsibility for their actions. The aim is to help teenagers grow into confident adults who are separate and independent but also appropriately connected to their family and able to form their own intimate relationships in the future.

A time of opportunity

While acknowledging the strife and difficulties involved in bringing up a teenager, this book also suggests that

parents seek out the positive and brighter side of parenting a teenager. Rather than seeing the teenage years as solely problem years, try to see them as full of opportunity. During these years parents have the opportunity to form a different relationship with their child, one that is more adult and equal. Teenage rebellion is not a personal attack on your authority but a necessary stage for teenagers to go through as they forge their separate identity. If you remain curious and interested in this process, you can help them think through their values and ideas. By staying involved in your teenagers' lives you can get to know them in a different light – as young adults rather than children. Many parents report how satisfying it can be to begin to have adult conversations with their teenagers. In addition, by staying involved you can share in their achievements and discoveries as they mature and grow up. You can appreciate and enjoy their excitement as they face a world full of opportunity and you can have the pleasure of being one of their closest supports as they take on the world. In the difficult times, try to remember that parenting is a long-term task. By staying involved and being firm when needed, you can chart a course through the difficult times so that you can be there as your teenagers grow into young adults of whom you can be proud.

Pressing the pause button in the face of conflict

It's the last straw for Pete when his fourteen-year-old son arrives home hours late after specifically promising to be in on time. Pete confronts him angrily, asking, 'Where the hell have you been?'. The son in return becomes defensive and angry and tells his father to mind his own business. The confrontation escalates and the son storms off to his room. Pete is left wondering what has happened between them.

Teenagers are at a time of life when they are separating from their parents. They are becoming their own people, with different ideas and values. Though this is healthy, it can bring them into conflict with their parents and lead to a stormy time for all. As we discussed in the last section, this period can be difficult for parents. Teenagers can become challenging and demanding. At times they can become disrespectful and even abusive to their parents. It is not surprising that parents, hurt and bewildered by these exchanges, can react negatively by criticising, lecturing, rowing and even lashing out at their teenagers. This can lead to unpleasant scenes, like that described above, leaving both teenager and parent upset and hurt.

So how can a parent handle this conflict? How can you stop things from escalating to a full-blown row? The first thing you can do is press the pause button. Rather than reacting to a situation or 'flying off the handle', pause and ask yourself the following questions:

1 What is the best way to manage this situation?

2   What way do I want to respond?

3   What result do I want?

In conflictual situations, pressing the pause button may mean taking a deep breath and calming down when you feel yourself getting angry or about to react to a situation. It can be best not to continue the argument, which may lead to hurtful things being said, and to set a time later to talk things through when everyone is calmer. Consider now how Pete in the example above might have pressed the pause button.

When his son came in late, Pete found himself getting very angry, but he quickly noticed this. He took a deep breath and said, 'Look son, I'm just too upset and angry to talk now. Go to your room and we will talk tomorrow'. The son went off in a huff, but a serious row was averted. Pete sat down and collected himself, thinking what was the best way to approach his son about his being late. He decided on a way and then sat down with him at a later time when both were calm.

When teenagers are disrespectful

Pressing the pause button can also be helpful when teen-agers become abusive and disrespectful to parents. Rather than tolerating the teenager's abuse or responding with a few choice words of your own, you can 'pause the row' by refusing to participate any more and waiting for a better time to resolve the conflict. Consider the example below:

> *When Alice asked her daughter to stay in one evening, she exploded abusively, telling her mother to 'back off' and 'stop messing up my life'. Though Alice was hurt and tempted to respond angrily, she pressed the pause button. She calmly said, 'Look, I'm not happy with you speaking to me in this way. When you can talk civilly, then I'll listen'. The daughter continued to protest and Alice repeated what she had just said and walked away. Away from the situation Alice thought about what to do and the daughter calmed down. An hour later her daughter approached her and the two of them sat down and talked. Alice calmly explained how hurt she was and the daughter apologised. Together they negotiated a compromise about going out.*

By pressing the pause button, Alice 'nipped the argument in the bud' and avoided the row escalating to a point where hurtful and damaging things were said. By not returning her daughter's abuse, Alice not only made it more likely that a more constructive conversation could take place later, but she also taught her daughter an important lesson about how to remain respectful and calm even in a difficult situation.

Don't wait for a row – press the pause button in advance!

As discussed at the beginning of this book, you don't have to wait until you are in the middle of a row to press the pause button and think through how you want to manage a conflict or how you want to be as a parent. In fact, the more often you sit down (either by yourself or with your partner or a trusted friend) to reflect on your parenting and to plan how you are going to handle situations, the better things are likely to be for yourself and your family. Good planning and communication can avoid many problems. For example, by taking time to plan with your

I'M NOT WAITING FOR A ROW – I'M PRESSING THE "PAUSE" BUTTON NOW!

SEE, MUM? I TOLD YOU YOU HAD NO PATIENCE!

teenagers the family holiday, a choice can be made that meets the preferences of everyone, and this can avoid resentment or a disastrous trip full of rows and conflict. However, many parents caught up in busy schedules forget to give themselves 'thinking time' or forget to plan things in their families. The purpose of this book is to 'press the pause button' in your busy parenting schedule and to give you 'thinking time'. Most of the exercises and suggestions in the book are about 'pausing' by yourself or with your children to think and talk about what way you want to be as a family.

Tips for going forward

1   Press the pause button when faced with rows and arguments. Step back and think how you want to respond.

2   Think of a particular problem in your family and decide how you want to respond to it.

Connecting with your teenager

When my children got older, I felt redundant. They had their own friends and lives. It became harder to understand them.

Parents matter

Often parents have the sense of being out of touch with their teenager. Teenagers get caught up with their own friends and interests, and it is easy to feel distant from them and that you don't matter to them any more. Yet teenagers still really need their parents. Though they are growing up and separating from the family, they still need support, guidance and encouragement. They need parents who remain involved and interested in their lives. Young people need adults who can be there to coach them and act as their 'co-pilot' as they negotiate the problems they face in their lives. If you are unsure about the importance of your role in your teenager's life, you only have to consider the extensive research showing that teenagers whose parents stay connected and supportively involved in their lives are much more likely to grow into healthy, successful adults with fewer problems. Researchers have also found that children whose parents discuss issues such as drugs with them are 36 per cent less likely to experiment with drugs than children whose parents do not have these discussions.

Staying involved in your teenagers' lives or having a connection with them does not mean knowing everything about them or learning things so you can control them. Teenagers need their privacy and distance and it would be inappropriate for them to reveal all their innermost secrets to their parents. Rather, having a connection with teenagers is about knowing the ordinary details in their lives that are important to them, such as the names of their friends, their routine at school, the position of their team in the league, what their favourite dinner is, etc. When you know these mundane and ordinary details about your teenagers' lives, not only does it mean that you are sharing in their lives, but it gives you an opportunity to influence them positively about other important matters such as drug-taking and safety.

Building a connection with your teenager

So how do you get through to teenagers? How do you reach out to them when they appear withdrawn and moody? This is often not easy, as there can be a great gap between parents and teenagers in terms of interests and concerns. Building a connection and a good relationship with your teenager takes effort and it is not something that can be done overnight, but rather is the result of careful emotional investment of time and energy. There are a number of ideas that can help.

Set time aside to be with your teenager

Building a connection with a child or teenager is not something that can be rushed or fitted into a busy schedule. The most important decision you can make is to set time aside when you can talk and be with your teenager in a relaxed way. This does not have to be a special activity or trip (though these can help, as we shall see in Step 3). Mundane, ordinary activities, such as watching TV together, driving to school, mealtimes, washing up together, all can become activities where parent and child are happily chatting to one another.

Rob found the drive to work in the morning when he dropped his son to school a real stress. They would always be late and tempers could be frayed in the traffic. As a result, he changed his schedule so as to have more time in the morning. This made the journey more relaxing, giving them time to spend together either chatting or listening to the radio. It became a time they both looked forward to.

Some parents find routine events of the day particularly helpful times to talk and listen to their children, such as when they come in from school, at mealtimes, or late at night just before they go to bed. Many families agree to make some of these times special, such as Sunday dinner, when everyone makes an effort to be there.

Get to know specific details about your teenager's world

Parents who are involved in their children's lives know countless ordinary details about their lives and what is important to them. They take an interest in their hobbies and make a point of remembering their friends' names. They are curious about what their children think and feel about things, especially things that are important to them. Gaining this knowledge of your child's life takes time but it really shows in the quality of interaction between parent and child. Consider the example below.

Joan would make a special effort to be available to her children when they came in from school. She would stop any work she was doing and sit down with her children over a cup of tea. She made sure there would be time and space for everyone to say how their day went. Joan made a point to ask specifically what went on for them during the day and she always remembered to ask about important things such as football matches or trips. This special time after school became a really important family ritual that Joan and the children looked forward to.

Be encouraging

Teenagers are often insecure and struggling with many pressures at school and from friends. The argumentative or sulky moods are only a front and they need more than ever the support and encouragement of their parents. It is important that this encouragement be given in a genuine way, as teenagers will be the first to shrug off any attention they consider to be 'phoney' or manipulative. Generally, encouragement works best with teenagers if it is matter of fact rather than 'over the top', and if it is specific and clear (whereby you clearly name what you are pleased about and how you feel about it). Remember, each teenager is different; what gets through with one teenager will not work for another. What is important is that you find a way of providing encouragement to your teenager about routine, everyday activities. Giving compliments to teen-agers in a genuine way that gets through to them can make a difference:

- noticing if your teenager tries harder at school work
- casually thanking your teenager when he does a chore, rather than taking it for granted

- complimenting teenagers on their appearance or what they're wearing

Going out of your way to look for positive things does not come easily to most of us. We are not used to it, and praise can be hard to give, particularly when there has been conflict or things have not been going well with a child for some time. But that is probably the most important time to be positive and to notice even small signs of improvement. For example, if your teenager is normally grumpy with visitors, but on one occasion, behaves more positively, you could say, 'I appreciate it when you talk with my friends, it means a lot to me when you take an interest'. Or if a teenager normally gets into a row with his sister, but on one occasion walks away, you could say, 'I was impressed with how you handled things with your sister earlier. You didn't get wound up and avoided a row'.

Responding to your teenager's initiative

One of the greatest opportunities to connect with teenagers is to respond to any initiatives they make to talk with or connect with you. Often they choose inopportune times, when you're busy or when you're tired or just about to go out and do something yourself. However, it's worth weighing up in these situations what is really important – the tasks you're busy with or your relationship with your teenager. While you can sometimes postpone responding to your teenager, it can be really helpful to respond there and then, especially if your teenager does not usually open up or try to make a connection with you. It can be a case of

making sure to 'seize the opportunity'. Consider the following examples:

- If your son asks for help with homework and you're busy, try to give a little bit of time and then set aside another time to help.
- If your daughter suddenly opens up one night because her boyfriend split up with her, this might be a time to postpone going to bed and to stay up and listen.
- If your son wants to watch a favourite TV programme and you're reading, it might be a good idea to postpone your reading and to watch the programme with him.
- If your daughter asks you a personal question when you're reading the newspaper, you can put down the newspaper for a few minutes and try to listen and answer the question.
- If your son asks you for a lift, rather than lecturing him about 'not being his chauffeur', use the journey as an opportunity to listen and talk to him.

Tips for going forward

1 Set aside a relaxed time to talk with your teenager, when the two of you can sit and chat.

2 Make a list of all the specific, mundane details you know about your teenager (friends, interests, school, likes/dislikes, etc.). Make an effort to fill any gaps you notice, by taking a real interest in your teenager's life next week (remember to 'go slow', as your teenager may only open up slowly).

3 Be really encouraging of your teenager. Go out of your way to notice any things he does that you like or you're proud of and make sure to tell him this.

4 Be sure to respond to any attempts your teenager makes to connect or talk to you.

Getting to know your teenager

Being a teenager

As a parent, it's easy to forget what it is like to be a teenager. You can find yourself being critical of the younger generation, complaining about their laziness or lack of respect for older people. You can just see their moodiness as a burden and something you can't understand. However, what young people really need is their parents' understanding. They are often very critical of themselves, feeling awkward and having low self-esteem. They need to know that you are on their side. To appreciate what it is like in your teenager's shoes, it can help to remember what it was like for you as a teenager when you were growing up. To do this, I suggest you take a few minutes with the following exercise.

Remembering being a teenager

1 Take a few moments out from your routine so that you can be alone, with time to think and reflect.

2 Close your eyes and take a few deep breaths to relax.

3 Begin to recall what it was like when you were ten or eleven years old. Pick out specific events or people that signify this time for you. Focus on recalling specific details (how you were feeling, what people were saying, what things looked like then, etc.).

4 When you're ready, begin to move forward in time to when you were fifteen or sixteen (in the middle of your teen years) and begin to recall what things were like for you then. Once again, recall specific events and people in as much detail as possible.

5 When you are ready, move forward again to the present day and back to the room you're in.

6 Think about what you noticed about your 'journey' through time. It can help to write things down in a journal or to talk to someone about what you have noticed or remembered, such as your partner. This can be a good exercise to do as a couple.

The above exercise can be very powerful in getting you in touch with your own teenage years. It can be a difficult exercise as you can recall sad memories, or it can be mixed as you recall good and bad memories. As a parent doing the exercise, it can make you realise some of the issues that your own teenager is going through. Though there are many differences between being a teenager nowadays and a generation ago (for example, it is true to say that teenagers have more freedom now and there is wider availability of drugs), many of the issues are the same. By remembering these common issues and concerns, you have made another step in understanding and connecting with your teenager.

What teenagers think about

So what do teenagers think about? What issues are important to them and what concerns press upon their minds? Below are the sorts of worries that teenagers have reported as most concerning them:

- Will I make friends or will anyone like me?
- Will anyone fancy me or ask me out?
- How come I don't fit in with others?
- What should I do about drugs and alcohol?
- Will I do okay in the class exams?
- Will I ever get a decent job?
- What should I do with my life?
- How can I please my parents/get them off my back?

Teenagers also tend to have strong views about how they should be parented and about what they want from their parents.

1 They want their parents to trust them and have faith in them.

2 They want privacy. They want to talk to their

parents about some things but they don't want to tell them everything.

3 They want to be treated fairly. Justice and fair play are really important to them.

Getting to know your teenager's world

As a parent, the best thing you can do to get alongside your teenager, so that you can be a positive influence in their life, is to go out of your way to understand them and to know their world. Rules and discipline require teenagers to cooperate voluntarily and thus are only possible when you have established a good relationship. Below are a number of things you can do to make a difference to your relationship with your teenager.

Be interested

Be genuinely interested in your teenagers and all they do. You want to know them, not because you want to control them, but because you genuinely want to get to know their world. You want to know their opinions, views and feelings. You want to understand why they love computer games so much, or what they see in football, so that you can share in this with them. This often requires suspending your critical judgements of their interests and hobbies and reaching out to understand them. For example, rather than always criticising a TV programme your daughter watches, make an effort to suspend judgement, watch it with her, and then debate the issues with her, listening to her point of view first. Let your teenager teach you about her interests and what it is like to be living in the teenage world. See yourself as a curious, respectful traveller in a foreign land (of adolescence!) rather than being a critical tourist! Rather than simply restricting your son's use of the Internet, let him teach you how to use it and show you the benefits and opportunities it provides. By learning about it yourself, you are in a better position to open a debate about the problems of safety or excessive use. You may be surprised to find that your teenager has already thought about many of the issues involved. Your job then becomes one of a supportive coach, helping him think things through further and make decisions.

Spend one-to-one time with your teenager

The best way to build a trusting close relationship with your teenager is to ensure that you have one-to-one quality time together, with no interruptions. While this can be difficult with teenagers who appear little interested in spending time with their parents, and when parents are busy with their own lives, time alone with your teenagers is still the best way to get to know them and stay involved with their lives. There are many things you can do to achieve this and often it is best to plan in advance to find activities that you enjoy doing together.

- watching a favourite TV programme
- doing homework
- shopping together
- playing cards
- playing sport
- baking/cooking
- walking the dog
- following a football team

- making something (i.e. a craft)
- walking, cycling
- camping
- doing a course together
- fishing
- working on the computer

Make a decision to get to know your teenager

Often getting to know your teenager isn't something that just happens. The generation gap can be quite large and requires an effort on the part of the parent to bridge it. This is especially the case when parents feel out of touch with their teenagers or if there has been a lot of conflict. Consider the two examples of parents below.

Richard found his fourteen-year-old son particularly grumpy and moody and he felt out of touch with him. So he looked to find an activity they could do together. The son was really interested in football, though Rob thought it was a waste of time. But he decided to take an interest in football and began to attend matches with his son. Slowly he discovered and began to share his son's love for the sport. The weekly football trip soon became their regular weekend outing and a real bond developed between them.

Sue found herself in constant battles with her daughter over school work. She was worried that they had nothing in common. However, when she thought about it she remembered that they both shared an interest in films. So as a treat she planned a special movie night, when the two of them would select a movie and go together, and round off the evening in a coffee shop. This worked well, as they always had a great chat about the movie and other things over coffee.

Be prepared to share your own experiences

Generally, teenagers love when parents are prepared to share their own honest feelings and experiences rather than just give lectures and advice. For example, rather than preaching to your son about the virtues of hard work in school or lecturing to him about the dangers of teenage sex, maybe share with him your own personal struggles in school or your own teenage worries about relationships and meeting the opposite sex. It can be helpful to share with your teenager the results of the remembering exercise at the beginning of this chapter. Sharing your own honest feelings and experiences can be really helpful in improving your relationship with your teenager. Consider the example from a mother below:

I was always concerned about my daughter not studying and going out all the time and this would lead to a lot of conflict. Things changed when we were away together one weekend and I told her honestly about my own school experience. I had been taken out of school early by my parents to work and always resented not having an opportunity to go to college. Talking to her made me realise how part of my pressure on my daughter was to do with my own lack of fulfilment. My daughter was very understanding when I told her this and she opened up about the pressures she had in school, which were different to mine. We began to understand one another and have been much closer as a result.

Spend family time together

Another way to get to know your teenager and to improve family life in general is to ensure that there are regular times when the whole family spends quality time together. This can include special activities such as a day-trip together, going on a picnic, or staying in for a special movie night. Many families organise a special family night (usually following a family meeting, see Part 1, Step 8) when everyone stays in, perhaps to share a meal together or a special family activity such as a game, telling stories, playing music, or simply spending time with one another.

Tips for going forward

1 Plan to do an activity or take up a hobby that you can share with your teenager.

2 Plan an enjoyable family event or set aside family time, which everyone, including your teenagers, can enjoy and take part in.

Empowering teenagers

As said before, parenting teenagers is a bit like teaching them to fly their own plane. During these years, the parent acts like a supportive co-pilot, ready to teach and support the 'trainee' pilot. Though it can be hard, you have to learn to relinquish the controls one by one and support your teenager as she learns to take responsibility. In addition, you have to remain sufficiently involved in your teenager's life so that she seeks out your support and accepts your influence. In other words, you may have to work very hard at staying connected with your teenager so that she allows you into the co-pilot's seat in the first place (and so that she doesn't later push the 'ejector button' and sack you from the role before the job is complete).

Just as the long-term aim of co-pilots is to empower their trainees to become fully qualified pilots, so the long-term aim of parents is to empower their teenagers to be confident, capable adults who are responsible for their own lives. However, this is more difficult than it seems, and many parents fall into the trap of being 'disempowering' rather than 'empowering' parents.

Disempowering parenting

Below are three styles of disempowering parenting that you can easily fall into, despite the best of intentions. Each of these styles cultivates irresponsibility in teenagers and does not prepare them for the task of being an adult.

1.   Over-protective parent

Doing everything for your teenagers, for example, waking them in the morning, making their breakfast and lunch, tidying up for them, washing their clothes, covering for them when they miss homework, etc.

2.   Critical parent

Nagging, correcting, instructing teenagers over every task without giving them space and responsibility – for example, nagging them to do the lawn and then standing over them while they do it, even criticising their attempts.

3. Permissive parent

Giving your teenagers excessive 'space' so that you are uninvolved and have little influence in their lives (meaning they learn little from you).

Empowering parenting

Be encouraging

Perhaps the most empowering thing you can do as a parent is to be supportive and encouraging. Begin to trust your teenagers and express your belief in their ability to succeed. Highlight and identify what they do right and the good qualities that they have. See yourself as a good coach in their lives. You cheerlead when they are successful, are a shoulder to cry on when they hit hard disappointments, and are there to chat to in the ordinary times. But you are always positively on their side. Even when they do wrong, you help them take responsibility, and you help them learn, but you continue to support and encourage them. Perhaps the greatest gift we can give our children is to maintain an unwavering belief in them during the bad times or periods of discouragement.

Let teenagers take responsibility for household and family tasks

This suggestion should be welcome relief to overburdened parents who do everything for their teenagers – you do them no service by taking charge of their lives in this way. It robs them of a chance to learn important life skills and to develop a sense of pride in carrying out the jobs well. Doing everything for teenagers also disempowers them, because it inadvertently communicates to them that they are not capable of carrying out the tasks in the first place. During the teenage years you should hand over household and family tasks to them one by one so that they eventually take a fair adult responsibility in the running of a home. Michael and Terri Quinn have compiled a list of all the tasks that parents could hand over to teenagers. They recommend using it as a checklist that you can review periodically to see what else you can hand over and teach your teenager.

TASKS TO TEACH YOUR TEENAGER

- weekly household shopping
- choosing their own clothes
- getting up in the morning
- washing-up
- mowing the grass
- painting a room
- paying bills
- locking doors at night
- cooking meals
- cleaning the house
- washing clothes
- ironing
- changing the oil in the car
- mending an electric fuse
- wiring an electric plug
- caring for a younger child
- cleaning the windows
- planting flowers and vegetables
- leading prayers
- chopping firewood
- settling their own squabbles
- doing basic repairs

Teach teenagers to make decisions in their own lives

Teaching teenagers to make decisions about their own lives is the most important task that parents can hand over. Parents should empower teenagers to begin to make decisions, such as how to manage their routine, what friends to have, what lifestyle to have, and what to do in the future. Rather than giving ready-made answers to these questions, it's best if parents step back and support teenagers in deciding for themselves. For example, if your son approaches you and asks you whether he should do French or History as an exam subject, it may be best for you not to give an immediate answer, but to ask, 'What do you think yourself?', or 'What do you think are the pros and cons for each subject?'. This way, you encourage your son to work out this decision for himself and prepare him for making adult decisions later on. Stepping back and letting teenagers evaluate decisions and consequences about their lifestyles can be difficult when you don't agree with some of their decisions. For example, it may be difficult to step back and listen first when your thirteen-year-old daughter says she wants to get her nose pierced, or if your fourteen-year-old son wants what you think is a crazy haircut.

Take time to teach your teenager

You can't suddenly hand over responsibility to teenagers without taking time to teach and prepare them for it. We often assume teenagers know how to do basic chores when no one has taught them. Just because they have watched you do the laundry or the ironing for many years doesn't mean they have learnt how to do it themselves. It takes skill, tact and time to teach someone something in a way

that empowers and motivates them. This is the difference
between nagging a child to mow the lawn, which they
eventually do badly, and teaching a child an appreciation
of gardening over time so that they mow the lawn better
than you and take pride in the result. In preparing children to take responsibility for a task, it can be helpful to
take time to:

1 Explain clearly what has to be done. Give them an
    appreciation of the purpose of the task.

2 Ask them what help they will need from you in
    order to learn the task (for example, you can demon-
    strate what has to be done, or you can do the task
    together, or you can let them go off and do the task
    and come back to you to report progress, or you can
    do all three in sequence).

3 As far as possible let them make choices in how the
    task is done. For example, you don't mind when
    your daughter does her ironing and washing, as
    long as it is not in the living room. For some tasks
    you can encourage your teenager to be creative (for
    example, on your son's night to cook, you let him
    surprise you with the menu).

4 Make your teenager accountable for the task, getting
    credit if it is done and experiencing consequences if
    not.

Allow teenagers to learn from consequences

Responsibility means experiencing the good and bad
consequences of our actions. Just as it is important to let

teenagers take credit for achievements and take pride in a job well done, it is also important to let them experience what happens when things go wrong, so they can learn from their mistakes. Parents can often rescue teenagers by covering for them when they don't do their homework, or giving them pocket money even though they did not complete the expected chore, or ironing their shirt at the last minute even though they can do it themselves. Letting teenagers experience consequences and learn from mistakes is not abandoning them; rather, it is teaching them to take responsibility for their actions. Even in doing this, you can still be encouraging and on their side, helping them learn; but you are not there to take over and rescue them. Consider the following example.

Thirteen-year-old Joe wanted to leave the football team. He didn't really enjoy it and just wanted out. Bob, his father, was worried. Joe didn't do much physical activity and didn't have many friends. He was worried that Joe would be 'moping around' the house, bored, for the summer. He listened to Joe, expressed his concerns, but Joe was adamant that he wanted to leave. In the end, Bob did not object but supported Joe in making his own decision. Sure enough, during the summer Joe began to complain that he was bored, that he had nothing to do and no friends to hang out with. Bob didn't react righteously with an 'I told you so' (though he felt like it); instead he bit his lip and empathised with how Joe was feeling. Being listened to, Joe was able to admit that he 'sort of regretted' leaving the football, though he still wanted to do something different. Bob told him that it took courage to face regrets and he asked Joe would he like some help in thinking what to do next. Joe readily agreed and together

*they found a different sports club that Joe made a
commitment to attend.*

Make teaching fun

Teaching a teenager a new task does not have to be boring
and formal. The more you make it fun and enjoyable, the
better. For example, you can ask your son to do a six-week
cookery course with you in the autumn; or offer to dec-
orate your daughter's room with her and use the time to
teach her painting skills; or you can suggest a family
spring-cleaning day (followed by a big family treat),
when each teenager chooses a special task but when you
all work together. Such shared activities are often times of
great connection between parents and children.

Start small

It can be a big transition to change to be an empowering
parent. If you are a parent who does everything for your
teenagers, it can be difficult suddenly to relinquish all
your jobs, and your teenagers doubtless would not be
prepared to take them on. It is best to start small and to
pick out something that you are going to teach your teenagers to do over the next week. Perhaps you are not going
to wash up every evening yourself but ask your children to
do a night each; or you're not going to take responsibility
to get them up every morning, or to do their laundry.
Whatever you decide, it's best to sit down and explain
in advance that you want to begin letting them take
some responsibility for household chores and family
tasks, explaining the benefits of this. Listen to their

ideas and views (you may be surprised that they are very
reasonable) and explain your own ideas and conclusions.
When you do start this new approach, expect some resist-
ance and teething problems. Teenagers may agree to do
tasks but find it hard to follow through and take responsibility. In addition, they are bound to test your word to
see if you really have changed, and it is important that you
keep your resolve. They need to discover that if they don't
do their own laundry, then nobody will magically step in,
and they really will have nothing to wear on Saturday
night.

Tips for going forward

1 Pick a family task or household chore that
you want to hand over to your teenagers.

2 Sit down and talk to them, explain why you
want to hand it over to them (e.g. a fairer
system, teaching them responsibility).

3 Agree to teach them the task if needed.

4 Agree on the rewards for doing the task and
the consequences for not.

5 Arrange to talk again to review how they got
on.

Communicating effectively

Listening and speaking up

Active listening

Most parents agree that listening to children is really important. Some writers in the field actually rate listening as the most important parenting skill of all. This is because it helps parents to both understand and get alongside their teenagers, and it also helps resolve conflict and carry out discipline firmly. Yet despite this, very few of us get any training in how to listen. It is something we just pick up as we go along, and sometimes we can find it very difficult, especially when we have strong views about what we want to happen for our teenagers.

Active listening involves great effort. It involves stepping out of your own shoes into those of another person. It involves moving to see the world as they see it and to appreciate the feelings they have towards it. It is about going that extra distance to understand their point of view. When faced by your child doing something you strongly disagree with, a good indicator that you have

understood empathetically is when you appreciate that you might have committed the same error if you had been in their shoes or faced their set of circumstances.

So how do you actively listen?

Active listening is very different from the many other ways we might communicate with teenagers, such as giving advice, criticising, or coaching (all useful skills at times, but not when we are actively listening to understand a child's feelings). Consider the following responses to a teenager:

> **Alison** (upset): *Gina* (an older sister) *is always saying nasty things about me.*

> **Parent:** *I'm sure she doesn't mean it* (coaching).
> *Well, that is because you are always calling her names too* (criticism).
> *Why don't you just ignore her* (advice).
> *Look, I will go and talk to her* (rescuing).

Instead, active listening is something quite different. It involves skills such as the following:

1 Genuinely trying to understand.

2 Acknowledging what the other person is feeling.

3 Repeating what the other person has said, to check you have understood.

4 Giving full attention via your body language and eye contact.

5 Encouraging the other person to continue by nodding, being silent, repeating the last word they have said, asking gentle questions, etc.

Consider now an alternative listening response:

Alison (upset): *Gina* (an older sister) *is always saying nasty things about me.*

Parent: *Sounds like you are upset. Sit down and tell me what happened* (picking up on feelings and encouraging teenager to say more).

Alison: *She is always having a go at me.*

Parent: *You feel she is always down on you* (trying to understand).

Alison: *Yeah, she told me in front of Rebecca* (a friend) *that she did not want me to hang round with them.*

Parent: *Ohh, that sounds hurtful.*

In the above examples the parent is validating the child's feelings and attempting to see the problem from her point of view. Sometimes, simply repeating what the child has said, or nodding encouragingly, can be sufficient to help the child feel listened to and to encourage her to express more.

It is important to remember that good listening can't be reduced to a set of techniques (if you do find yourself 'parroting' techniques, your teenager will soon point this out to you). What counts is your genuine attempt to understand and appreciate the other's point of view. You have listened effectively when the other person feels understood, that you don't judge them, and that you are on their side.

Listening changes you

When we empathetically listen to another person we open ourselves to be influenced by them. We allow ourselves to be changed and transform the nature of our relationship with the other person. Consider the following example from a father.

> I always considered myself to have a good relation-ship with my two teenage sons. I thought everyone enjoyed the joking and good-natured banter that would go on between us. That was until the young-est of the two exploded one day over very little. I gave him what for, but I could see something was really bugging him so I went back to him and lis-tened. He told me how he had always felt embar-rassed and humiliated by the banter and the teasing.

I began to hear how this had really damaged him. I can't tell you how painful this was to hear. But it marked a pivotal point in our relationship. One year on we now have a much closer and adult relationship. I am really glad now that I decided to listen that day.

Speaking up

We've talked about the importance of actively listening to teenagers when they feel strongly about something. It is equally important that parents communicate their own feelings when they feel strongly about something. Teenagers need parents who don't go along with everything they say or who always agree with them. They need parents who are prepared to state their own views and to communicate their values and opinions. How this is done makes a big difference. Skilled communicators always listen first before speaking up with their own point of view. Often people get the order of this the wrong way round: they attempt to get their point of view across before listening to the other person. This can lead to a lot of conflict. When we understand another person's

point of view and have acknowledged their feelings, they are far more likely to be open to listen to us. Expressing your views and concerns also requires skill and tact. Often parents fall into the traps of blaming, criticising or not acknowledging their own feelings. Speaking up respectfully involves:

1 Remaining calm and positive.

2 Taking responsibility for your feelings by using an 'I' message, for example, 'I feel upset' rather than 'You made me upset'.

3 Expressing your positive intentions and concerns, such as 'I want you to be safe'.

4 Focusing on what you want to happen, for example, saying, 'I want you to tell me when you're late'.

Examples of ineffective and effective speaking up

Ineffective: *What the hell are you playing at, staying out so late? You've really upset me* (attacking and blaming 'you' message).

Effective: *I worry about you going out late at night, especially when it is dark. You see, I want you to be safe* (expresses feelings as a positive concern using an 'I' message).

Ineffective: *Is there something wrong with you that you don't see this mess? You and your friends are so inconsiderate* (sarcastic, blaming).

Effective: *Listen, I like it when your friends come round, but I get frustrated if they leave the place in a mess. I'd really like it if they tidied up after themselves* (states positive first, acknowledges own feelings of frustration and then makes a clear reasonable request).

Ineffective: *You're talking rubbish now. Of course it's always wrong for teenagers at school to get involved in a sexual relationship* (argumentative, attacking).

Effective: *My own view is that teenagers at school are far too young to get involved in a sexual relationship* (respectful offering of parent's view/value).

Tips for going forward

1 Practise communicating well with your teenagers and other family members. When they feel strongly about something, make a real attempt to actively listen and to understand their point of view.

2 Practise speaking up respectfully to your teenagers, offering your view in a calm, assertive way.

Managing conflict

Fifteen-year-old Lisa arrives home from school one day to drop the bombshell to her father, Bill, that she's had enough and that she has decided to leave school. Bill, who is just home after a stressful day at work, flies off the handle saying she's talking nonsense, that she is far too young even to consider leaving school. Lisa storms off, slamming a door, saying she's going to leave anyway.

Conflicts such as the one described above are common in families with teenagers or older children. Teenagers are on the road to becoming independent from their parents and this can be a long process, with each 'step of independence' being hard-won as parent and child clash over rules. Adolescence is the time of life when young people need to separate and be different from their parents – they will often have different views on clothes, time-keeping, friends, money, the importance of school work. Though it can lead to conflict, the expression of these different views

is healthy and helps young people grow up into confident adults.

What is important is how conflict is managed in families. You want to have a family in which there is a healthy and respectful expression of differences, but you do not want excessive conflict, leading to constant rows, as this can make things worse and damage relationships. In this chapter we look at how, as a parent, you can manage conflict between yourself and your teenager in a way that is respectful and positive and that offers the possibility of resolving the disagreements that caused the problems in the first place. We review ideas already covered in the book, especially in the previous chapter (Part 2, Step 5), and consider how these can be applied specifically to re-solving conflict.

1 Pressing the pause button.

2 Active listening.

3 Speaking up assertively.

Pressing the pause button

The behaviour of teenagers can be very provocative and challenging at times. In working out their own views, teenagers may reject values or ideas that are very important to their parents. For example, if you are a religious person, your teenager may refuse to go to church, or if cooking is important to you, your teenager might reject your food and choose an 'alternative diet', or if education is important to you, your teenager may threaten to drop out of school. Teenagers can know what buttons to push to get you going and this can cause great conflict. However, the first step to combat this is to press your own pause button. Rather than reacting angrily, take some time out to understand what is going on. Instead of taking your teenagers' behaviour personally, understand it as part of their growing up into being adults. Remember, if you do resort to lecturing or angry exchanges, you may inadvertently fan the flames of the rebellion.

Pressing the pause button gives you time to think through the best way to respond. Even if there has been a row or if you have over-reacted, pressing the pause button gives you an opportunity to apologise and start again. In the example at the beginning of this chapter, Lisa's father, Bill, could recover after the row, by taking some time for himself to reflect about what was going on, then to approach Lisa later at a good time, apologising for 'flying off the handle', and finally to ask her to start again and tell him what happened.

Active listening

In conflict situations between parent and teenager, emotions are likely to be running high. Conflicts are at their strongest when both parent and teenager feel really strongly, but differently, about something. In the above example, Lisa may be feeling really hopeless about her school, thinking it has no benefit to her. Her father on the other hand may believe strongly that teenagers should finish school and may feel scared at the prospect of her leaving early. In the context of their strong but different feelings, it is understandable that Bill may get angry and Lisa may storm off. However, until they find a way of listening to one another, they are unlikely to resolve the disagreement.

Active listening isn't easy. It is especially hard when there is serious conflict such as that between Bill and Lisa. However, these are the times when active listening is especially useful. If you don't listen, the conflict doesn't disappear, in fact it may worsen, as your teenager is likely to feel hurt and to close up and not tell you what is really going on with her. Consider the above example, now continued below, where Bill goes out of his way to listen to Lisa's feelings and to understand her point of view:

Bill (pauses and takes a deep breath): *Look, I'm sorry, let me try to understand.*

Lisa: *School is wrecking my head. I'm always in trouble. Even when I try, the teachers don't notice.*

Bill: *I see.*

Lisa: *Yeah, each day I go in I feel they're picking on me. I'd be better off leaving and getting work.*

Bill: *You've been having a real hard time at school recently.*

Lisa: *Yeah I have.*

(Father silently nods and puts arm around daughter's shoulder, who shows a small response, suggesting she is beginning to feel understood.)

Lisa: *That's why I want to leave. I'd be much better leaving and getting a job somewhere* (pause).

Bill: *Mmmh, I don't think I've appreciated how much of a struggle school has been for you, I guess, because I've always wanted it to go well for you. I need to think about what you are saying. Can we talk later, because it is a very important issue?*

Lisa: *Yeah.*

In the above conversation, Bill is making a real attempt to listen to his daughter, but it is hard for him. It is hard for him to take on board his daughter's struggles in school and thus her wish to leave, probably because these views run counter to his strongly held opinion about the importance of completing education. However, if he truly wants to support his daughter's education, he first has to become her ally. He first has to hear about his daughter's difficulties in school before he can go on to help her solve the problem. (In Step 8 we will look at possible ways of developing solutions.)

When your teenager feels strongly about something, these are really opportunities in disguise. By really listening at these times, you have the opportunity to deeply connect with your teenager and to transform your relationship with her.

Speaking up assertively

While listening is usually the best way to start during a conflict, it is also important for parents to speak up and communicate their own point of view. However, the way this is done makes a real difference. It is important not to come across as aggressive, where you intimidate or inadvertently attack your teenager. Equally, it is important not to be passive, where you don't get your view across for fear of upsetting your teenager, or you back down too easily and let your teenager walk all over you. Rather, the aim is to speak up assertively, whereby you communicate respectfully and calmly what you feel and think, making sure to express your positive intentions and feelings.

Even during serious conflicts and problems between parent and child, active listening and speaking up assertively are the best ways to begin to resolve them. Consider the next example, where a mother tackles her son over the drugs she has found in his room. She has taken time to think about what she is going to say and has picked a good time to approach her son to discuss what she has found.

Mother: *Look, I've something very important to talk to you about.*

Son: *What?*

Mother: *I found this in your room* (puts what looks like cannabis on the table; son looks shocked).

Mother: *I know it is cannabis.*

Son (outraged): *What the hell were you doing in my room?*

Mother (calm): *I was worried because of what the teacher said about you using drugs, so I decided to check.*

Son: *You had no right to go into my room.*

Mother (respectfully): *I'm sorry I had to, but I needed to check what the teacher said.*

Son (slumps in chair): *Well, it's none of your business.*

Mother: *It's because I'm very worried for you. I don't want you to use drugs.*

Son: *It's only hash. It's no big deal.*

Mother: *It is a big deal to me. I want you to be safe and well.*

(Teen folds arms.)

Mother: *Listen to me.* (Teen turns.) *We are going to have to talk about this and sort it out.*

(The son sighs and sort of gives in, as if he's beginning to sense his mother's persistent concern for him.)

In the last example the mother spoke up firmly and well. She had clearly thought through what she was going to say. Though it was a serious and worrying issue, she remained calm. She expressed her feelings clearly and positively, stating her concern for her son. Finally, she did not take the bait in rising to her son's anger and was persistent in getting her positive message through.

In summary

Managing conflict is essentially about good, respectful communication. It is about making sure you are talking and discussing things openly, rather than simply fighting and arguing. It is about staying involved and appreciating differences and not withdrawing or avoiding conflict. The two most important communication skills are listening empathetically and speaking up respectfully. You want to understand the other person's point of view and help them understand you as well. Remember these two skills form the building blocks of resolving disagreements and when applied over time can resolve even the most serious conflict.

Tips for going forward

When you find yourself in a dispute next week, practise (1) pausing rather than reacting, (2) active listening before you respond, (3) respectfully speaking up and giving your point of view.

Negotiating rules and boundaries

One evening fifteen-year-old Paul tells his parents that he wants to stay over at his friend Bill's house for the forthcoming Halloween night. His parents, who have only met Bill twice, are unsure, and they tell Paul they want to speak to Bill's parents first. Paul doesn't want this, saying it would be 'humiliating'. He wants his parents to trust him instead.

What decisions should teenagers make for themselves and what rules and boundaries should parents establish? What are reasonable rules to have for teenagers and how do you enforce them in a way that teaches self-responsibility?

This chapter gives some suggestions as to how parents might negotiate and follow through on rules with their teenagers, a process that, when handled correctly, can teach a young person responsibility and build mutual respect between parent and child. We build on all the valuable skills already covered (such as pressing the

pause button, listening during conflict and speaking up assertively) and add three further important stages:

1   Negotiating and agreeing rules.

2   Agreeing on consequences.

3   Following through.

Negotiating and agreeing rules

Remember the 'big picture'

Parenting is a very long-term task. The goal is to help teenagers to learn how to be responsible adults who confidently make their own decisions. Rules should be seen as a flexible set of guidelines and agreements that are established to help navigate this long parenting journey. Good rules allow children to take responsibility for their actions and to learn from their mistakes. You don't want a set of rules that over-controls a young person, meaning that they never learn things for themselves. Nor do you want no rules or boundaries at all so that a young person is exposed to unnecessary risk and has few guidelines to learn from. You want rules that protect young people, but that also let them learn and begin taking more responsibility for themselves.

Involve young people in deciding family rules

Negotiate, negotiate and negotiate. These are the three most important principles in agreeing rules with teenagers. The more they are involved in the discussion, the more you listen to them, the more you try to accommodate their views and wishes, the more likely they are to respect and uphold the rules. The process of negotiation can take a lot of time. It involves lots of discussions, lots of one-to-ones and possibly lots of family meetings. Busy parents can often be tempted just to impose a rule or make a quick decision. However, this overlooks the benefits of negotiation. The process of negotiation ensures that you as a parent remain appropriately involved in your teenagers' lives. It gives you a chance to connect with them and to communicate your own values and feelings. In addition, it teaches young people how to express themselves and to think through their own opinions and values. It is certainly worth the time.

Rules work best when they are family agreements that everyone was involved in creating and that everyone tries to keep. For example, if you're concerned as a parent about the amount of TV your kids watch, rather than simply imposing a rule such as 'No TV before 6 p.m.', why not spend some time (perhaps in a family meeting – see Step 8) discussing the issue, highlighting the benefits and dangers of TV, and try to come to an agreement? Remember, this could take time and lots of listening (and several meetings!), but if you arrive at an agreement,

you have achieved a priceless piece of work in teaching
responsibility.

Keep 'non-negotiable' rules to a minimum

Parents often make the mistake of having too many rules
for their teenagers, which can lead to conflict and rob
teenagers of the chance of making their own decisions.
For example, do you really have to insist that your
daughter tidies her room to your standards or can you
close the door and let her take responsibility? Or you
may not like your son's haircut, but maybe it's best not
to make an issue of it, and let him decide how to cut his
hair. While there are times when you have to make rules
that your teenager doesn't agree with, these should be
kept to a minimum and reserved for really important
things. It helps to think through in advance what rules
are really important to you as a parent. Often families sit
down and come up with these together. Such 'non-
negotiable' rules might include:

- no drug-taking
- letting you know where they are
- not travelling alone at night
- friends welcome, but only when an adult is in the
  house

Even when you do make a rule that your teenagers are
unhappy about, it is still important to talk it through
with them and to listen to their point of view and feelings.
In addition, teenagers can be helped to accept a rule when
they are given choices about how it is enforced. In the
example at the beginning of the chapter, the father

could help fifteen-year-old Paul to accept the rule by giving the following choice:

> *I'm sorry Paul, but if you want to stay over at your friend Bill's house, then I want to ring his parents first to check it's OK. I understand that you find this a bit embarrassing but I need to know you will be safe. You may want to tell his parents first that I'm going to ring if that is easier for you – that's your choice – but I need to talk to them before you go.*

Agreeing on consequences

You won't be surprised to hear that even though you can reach well-thought-out agreements about rules with your teenagers, they will still break them. The route to self-responsibility involves lots of challenging and testing of limits. For this reason, it is best to have thought through in advance the consequences of rules being broken and agreements not being respected. These work best if they are reasonable and fair and if the teenager has been involved in deciding them. Discussing consequences with teenagers in advance gains their cooperation and treats them as accountable adults. Ask your teenagers what they think should be the fair consequence of breaking a rule or an agreement. You may be surprised that they will generate better and more effective examples than what you thought of yourself. Examples of consequences include:

● If Rob is an hour late coming in, then he has to be in an hour earlier the next night.

- If Sue does not do her chores for the week, then either she has to do double chores the next week or she doesn't get her pocket money for the week.
- If James does not arrive home for a family dinner, then no cooked meal is available for him.
- If Orla does not get up early enough, then she has to walk to school without a lift.
- If Peter does not do his washing and ironing, then he has no clean clothes on Saturday.
- If the washing-up rota is not working, you will discuss it again at the next family meeting.

The last consequence is a particularly important one. If the agreement is not working then it will be discussed again rather than forgotten about and abandoned. Knowing that there is a review time, when they will be accountable to other family members, is a powerful motivating factor for teenagers to 'get their act together' and to do what they promised. The style of the meeting should be exploratory and not punitive. The aim is to understand what happened and brainstorm how to move forward to solve the problem.

Even with serious problems, establishing consequences with teenagers can help them take responsibility for their actions. Often these consequences can be given as choices to teenagers. For example:

Parent: *I can't sit by and let you use drugs with your friends. I'm too concerned about you. Either you choose to stop meeting your friends at the club or you come with me to see the drugs counsellor.*

Parent: *If you get suspended from school, then you stay in at home and study for the period you are suspended. You won't be allowed out or to play computer games.*

Following through

Following through is essentially about you as a parent keeping the promises and agreements you have made with your teenagers, so that they learn to do likewise. It is about not giving in and ironing your son's shirt for him at the last minute because you feel sorry for him, or taking your daughter in the car when she's late for school, when you agreed before that she should take responsibility. Keeping these promises can be hard on parents, which makes it important only to make agreements and consequences that you know you can keep yourself.

When following through, it is best not to make a fuss about it or use it as an opportunity to lecture your teenager, for example, 'I knew you would not be able to get up on time – it is typical.' Instead, try to be calm, firm and matter of fact. You can even be supportive, but do not rescue. For example, it is okay to say when your son misses an agreed family meal, 'I'm sorry you're hungry', but it would be a mistake to make him a special meal.

In addition, if you agree that a rule (e.g. a chore rota) will be reviewed at a later date, for example, at a family

meeting, it is important that this meeting does in fact take place and that you don't avoid the discussion for fear of upsetting your teenagers or inviting trouble. By keeping your side of the bargain, you model responsibility and make teenagers accountable for their actions.

Tips for going forward

1 Make a list of the really important rules you want kept in your house (this can be a great exercise to do with the whole family).

2 Negotiate the exact form of these rules with your teenagers and what the consequences are when rules are not kept.

3 Be sure to follow through on any consequences you agree.

Solving problems/ Talking things through

The secret to getting along with your teenagers and reducing conflict is in finding better ways of communicating
with them – finding ways to listen and to get through to
them. While this is true of all children, it is especially true
of teenagers, who are developing more of an adult relationship with their parents. Most of the ideas in this book
have been geared towards improving communication
within families. Good communication is the basis for
solving problems. Connecting with teenagers, finding
out about their worlds, listening and speaking to them
in the good times, give a basis for talking things through
and solving problems during the rough times.

Solving problems

The mark of a healthy family is not whether they have
problems or not, but whether they go about trying to

solve them. What counts is being able to sit down and talk through the problems as they arise. Once a family is able to do this they can get through most of the difficult times they encounter. Below is a six-stage model you can use to solve problems. This model can be used (1) during a family meeting when everyone is present, or (2) with an individual child, or (3) with your partner when you have a difference of opinion, or (4) even by yourself to think through a dilemma you have. The six stages are:

1 Connecting/setting time and space aside.

2 Listening first.

3 Speaking up respectfully.

4 Thinking up solutions.

5 Choosing the best solutions/making agreements.

6 Meeting again/follow-up.

The first three stages have already been covered, and indeed the basic skills of connecting with teenagers –

listening first and speaking up respectfully – are often sufficient in themselves to solve problems. This is especially the case with listening. The source of most conflict between parents and teenagers is misunderstanding and lack of trust. Once this is resolved through empathetic listening, much of the conflict dissolves and solutions can naturally flow. Stages 4 to 6 describe how solutions and agreements can be established.

Thinking up solutions

Once you have understood your teenager's point of view and expressed your own feelings, you are now in a position to think up or 'brainstorm' with her possible solutions to the problems you are facing. Rather than simply giving your own solutions it is important to hold back and first encourage your teenager to come up with ideas and ways forward herself. This can be done by asking questions such as: 'How do you think you can solve this?', 'How can you ensure you get home on time?', and 'How can you convince the teachers that you're trying a little harder?'. Though it is tempting to come up with your own answers, it is crucial to proceed at the teenager's pace and to wait for her to generate the solutions. Solutions generated by teenagers are far more likely to be carried through by them. You will be surprised at how even the most 'difficult' teenager, when given time, can come up with solutions that are as good as or even better than those thought up by parents. Parents can add their own ideas and suggestions, but this is best done after your teenager's ideas have been explored or when she specifically asks you for suggestions.

At the brainstorming stage it is important to generate as many alternative solutions as possible – the more you have the better. It is also important not to be critical at this stage; encourage your teenager's creativity and listen to all the ideas she comes up with. These can include solutions tried successfully in the past. You can help your teenager recall times when things were going better or the problem was solved. For example, you can ask, 'How have you solved this in the past?', or 'Do you remember last year we had the same problem? But we got through it. How did we do it then?' Once talked about and understood, these past solutions are more easily repeated.

Choosing the best solutions/ making agreements

Now it is time to help your teenager decide which solutions she is going to use. During this stage the emphasis is on helping teenagers think through the consequences of the ideas suggested in the brainstorming stage, in order to identify those that have the best results for both them and other people. Frequently, teenagers come up with unrealistic or inappropriate solutions. However, rather than criticising, you can guide them by asking them to think of the consequences. Asking questions like 'What do you think will happen if you try that?' can be helpful. For example, as a way of avoiding a bully, a teenager might suggest dropping out of the school team. But on thinking it through, he realises that this could leave him feeling like a failure and would mean him losing out on being part of the club. With the support of his parent he may come up with a different solution, such as confronting the bully or gaining the support of the other boys to do something about it.

Meeting again/follow up

When the best solution(s) is/are chosen, it is important to arrange a time to talk again to review how things are going. This is a crucial and often-forgotten stage. Solving problems takes time and often many attempts, and persistence is needed to make a breakthrough. If an attempted solution doesn't work out, it is important to meet again to find out what happened and to support your teenager in finding a new course of action. Even if things do work out, meeting again gives you a chance to encourage and compliment your teenager, and this can be very empowering to them. In addition, by meeting again and thus following up on agreements, you make your teenagers (and yourself) accountable and thus encourage them to take responsibility for their actions.

Problem-solving in action

Let's look at how this problem-solving model can work. We will continue the example introduced in Step 5, where fifteen-year-old Lisa is discussing with her father, Bill, the idea of leaving school. After initially flying off the handle, Bill pressed the pause button and set aside a time to talk to Lisa. He first listened as she spoke of her struggles in school, and then he expressed his concerns about her leaving early. In the dialogue below, they go on to look at possible solutions.

Brainstorming/thinking up solutions

Bill: *I just wonder, if things were a little different at school, would you be able to turn things around?*

Lisa: *I don't know.*

Bill: *Well, what would help?*

Lisa: *Well, it's mainly Irish and History that I get into trouble in.*

Bill: *Maybe we could look at getting extra help for those classes.*

Lisa: *Or maybe I could get out of doing them altogether, and just concentrate on the others.*

Bill: *Maybe, we'd have to talk to the principal about that ... What could you do to help?*

Lisa: *Well, I could try to keep out of trouble and to work harder.*

Bill: *That might help.*

Lisa: *I also still wonder whether I would be better leaving and getting an apprenticeship.*

Bill: *That is another possibility.*

Lisa: *Or if I did leave, maybe I could study at home and still do the exams.*

Bill: *Possibly.*

Notice how at this crucial stage Bill encouraged Lisa to come up with solutions herself. He did not criticise her ideas, but encouraged her to identify as many potential solutions as possible. The aim at this stage of problem-solving is to be creative and to work with your teenager to generate lots of ideas and possibilities.

Choosing the best solutions

Bill: *So we've got a few ideas then. We could try to get you extra help for the classes, or talk to the principal about reducing the time you spend in some classes, and you could think of how to keep out of trouble and work a bit harder. Or you could look at leaving school at some stage and either seeking a job, or maybe doing the exams while at home. What do you think?*

Lisa: *I'll try to give it another go at school. Maybe we could talk to the principal, but I'm not sure it will work.*

Bill: *We can still look at the other options. It's probably a good idea that you look at what you want to do when you leave school anyway – whether this is sooner or later. It would be good if you could leave with some exams.*

Reviewing how you get on

Bill: *How does that sound?*

Lisa: *Okay.*

Bill: *We'll talk again about it next week.*

While in real life problem-solving may take a lot longer, especially for a difficult issue (and that is why it is crucial for Bill to meet Lisa to talk again), the above example illustrates the different steps you can take to talk through problems with young people.

Family meetings

As discussed in Part 1 of this book, family meetings are an excellent way of not only providing a forum to discuss and solve problems but also of ensuring families stay connected and have fun together. Family meetings, however, can be difficult to establish, especially with teenagers who are initially suspicious or cynical about the process. Drawing a teenager into participating can take time but it is well worth the effort.

Drawing teenagers into family meetings

1. INTRODUCE THE MEETING AS IMPORTANT BUT INFORMAL

Rather than making the meeting sound very 'formal', it can be helpful to introduce it in a matter-of-fact, informal way – for example, 'I thought it would be a good idea if we could all have a meal together on Thursday. It would also give us time afterwards to discuss the summer holidays. I want to hear your views on where we should go'.

NEXT TIME IT'S YOUR TURN TO HOST THE FAMILY MEETING!

2. MAKE MEETINGS RELEVANT TO THEIR CONCERNS

Make sure the meetings address issues that matter to the teenagers (as well as issues that matter to you). For example, if your daughter says she feels she's lumbered with all the household chores, or your son approaches you saying he wants a TV in his room, rather than solving these disputes there and then, say, 'Why don't you bring it up at the next family meeting?' If these are issues that they feel strongly about, they are likely to attend and participate.

3. SHARE POWER DURING THE MEETING

Attending family meetings is usually attractive to teenagers once they see that it is a forum where they will get a 'fair hearing' and can have an input in how family decisions are made. For this reason, share out power in the meeting. Encourage teenagers to take the role of chair or note-taker from time to time.

In addition, 'go slow' during meetings. Decisions can be postponed until the next meeting if there is not enough time. The main focus is on listening and understanding, making sure everyone has a chance to air their views.

4. MAKE MEETINGS FUN AND NOT ALL WORK

A lot of families end their meeting with a game or a special family activity that everyone enjoys. Children can be given turns in selecting the activities.

5. DON'T MAKE MEETINGS COMPULSORY

Don't get into a power struggle, forcing a teenager to attend a family meeting, as this can defeat the purpose. Instead, strongly encourage them to attend, making it attractive for them to do so. Let them experience the consequences if they don't attend, for example, not being there when important decisions affecting them are made, missing out on a favourite meal and a fun time.

6. PERSIST WITH DRAWING THEM IN

Don't worry if teenagers come with an 'attitude' or appear little interested from time to time, which is quite normal. Instead, persist with respectful communication on your part. Even the most 'switched off' teenager can open up eventually and participate.

Tips for going forward

1 Set aside a time to talk through a problem with your teenagers using the six-stage model described in Step 8.

2 Rather than immediately giving solutions, remember to hold back and to help teenagers generate their own solutions. Listen to their ideas first and add yours later.

RENEWAL AND RESOURCES

Parents caring
for themselves

There was a man working furiously in the woods trying to saw down a tree. He was making very little progress as his saw was blunt and becoming blunter with each stroke. The man was hot and frustrated and continued to work harder and harder. A friend of his noticed what was going on and he asked him, 'Why don't you stop for a few minutes so you can sharpen your saw?'. 'Don't you see,' replied the man, 'I'm too busy sawing to take any time off.'

Stephen Covey uses the above story to illustrate the futility of working non-stop and the importance of parents taking time off for rest and relaxation to renew themselves. So many parents become martyrs to their children, devoting all their time and energy to the task of parenting, without thinking of their own needs and wishes. Other parents become excessively focused on the problems and conflicts they have with their children and all their energy is spent in disagreeing with their children or correcting and rowing with them. In both these positions, not only is the parent liable to 'burnout' from stress and exhaustion, but their parenting becomes increasingly counter-productive and negative. In the first example, the parents can become resentful and/or can become run down, with little energy to relate to their children in a consistent, loving way. In the second example, the correcting approach is liable to increase the power struggle between parent and teenager, and may lead to more rebellion, until either the parent gives up or the teenager walks out.

As the story above suggests, it is crucial to take time out to 'sharpen the saw'. Parents should 'press the pause button' and take time to look after their own needs as well as attending to the needs of their children. When parents' own needs for care, comfort and fulfilment are met, they are freed up to attend fully to the parenting role. Children need cared-for parents as much as they need parents to care for them. The best way to help your children grow up to be confident people with high self-esteem is for you as their parent to model this – that is, to take steps to value, love and prioritise yourself.

You may protest that in your busy life you simply can't afford to take time out for yourself. The reality is that you can't afford not to. Think about the times you have been run down or exhausted or feeling low and how it was impossible then to do any of the 'more important' tasks. Remember the times you felt energetic and good about yourself and how easy it was then to achieve things and to be kind and loving to others. A little a bit of self-care goes a long way.

How to sharpen the saw

Self-care and personal renewal are basically about achieving balance in your life. They are about trying to ensure each week that you address your different needs in a balanced way. There are four dimensions of self-care and personal renewal that we need to address weekly in order to have a balanced and stress-free life.

1. PHYSICAL

- exercise (such as walking, jogging, playing sports)
- eating well and healthily
- getting good rest and relaxation

2. MENTAL

- keeping your mind stimulated with other interests (such as reading, movies, theatre, etc.)
- learning new things

3. EMOTIONAL

- keeping in contact with friends
- connecting with intimate family (e.g. special night out with partner)
- doing self-nurturing things (e.g. treating yourself to a special bath or a shopping trip)

4. SPIRITUAL

- time alone/time in nature
- time for personal reflection
- meditating, prayer
- goal-setting, reconnecting to your values.

The aim of self-care is look after your greatest asset in creating a happy family life – you. All the ideas in this book can only work when a vibrant, motivated and cared-for parent is there to implement them. Caring for yourself as a parent is really the first, or the most integral step in making a difference to your relationship with your children and teenagers.

Family renewal

Taking time out to sharpen the saw is something that applies equally to family life. Healthy families find time to renew and recharge themselves. Much of what has been described in this book is all about renewing and rebuilding family relationships. For example, we have described connecting and sharing with family members, spending quality relaxed and enjoyable times with one another, listening empathetically, and expressing our own feelings. All these activities 'sharpen the saw', for individual family members and for the family as a whole. Ensuring you have regular quality time, by yourself, with your partner, with your children and with your family as a whole, can be a way of not only eliminating stress but also of finding personal meaning and making the roller coaster ride of parenting an enjoyable one.

Tips for going forward

1 Set aside a special time next week, just for yourself, doing something you really enjoy.

2 Plan to spend special relaxed time with your partner away from problems next week. If you are a single parent, do the same with a close friend or other family member.

Seeking further help and support

This book has been written as a 'self-help' resource for parents. My aim has been to provide you with information that can empower you in the valuable and important job of bringing up children. This is not to say that parents don't need lots of support. Parenting works best when you have lots of ongoing support from other people (such as extended family and friends) and access to special support and services when faced by special difficulties. For this reason, it is important that you do seek further help as and when you need it.

A critical source of support is often from your child's teacher or child-minder. Many of children's problems occur in school, as do many of the solutions. It is important that you work in partnership with your children's teachers. A lot of research studies have shown that children do best when their parents are closely involved in their education and have good working relationships with their teachers. In addition, by working with the school you can often gain extra supports for your child, for example, educational psychology, remedial

help, after-school services. The school is often the first
port of call in gaining extra help for your child.

In addition, you can seek help from other professional
services such as the health visitor or baby nurse when your
child is young, or your family GP. Most areas have a child
and family centre or a family resource centre or a variety
of playgroups and parents groups which can provide lots
of helpful services to you and your children. Do check out
what resources are available in your local area. Finally,
you might find it useful to do a parenting course or to
join a parenting group. Many parents find it immeasur-
ably helpful to meet other parents in similar situations,
gaining support and new ideas. Parenting groups are very
common and are often run from your local family resource
centre or school, or even the local adult education centre.
The addresses and websites below can provide you with a
starting point as you search for information about the
services that best suit you. The essential thing is to
make sure you get out there and get the help you need.
Good luck!

Useful helplines, websites and addresses

UK

Childline
Advice line: 0800 11 11
Web: www.Childline.org.uk

Department for Education and Skills (DfES)
(*Parental advice on their children's education*)
Web: www.dfes.gov.uk/parentsgateway/index/shtml

Fathers Direct
(Provides information relevant to fathers and
practitioners working with fathers)
Herald House, 15 Lamb's Passage, Bunhill Row, Greater
London, EC1Y 8TQ
Tel: 020 7920 9491.
Email: enquiries@fathersdirect.com
Web: www.fathersdirect.org

For Parents by Parents
(*Internet support of one another, information and advice site
for parents, directory of Web pages for help and advice*)
Email: contributions@forparentsbyparents.co.uk
Web: www.forparentsbyparents.com

Full Time Mothers
(*A voluntary organisation, parent support group and
campaign network*)
Full Time Mothers, PO Box 186, London, SW3 5RF
Tel: 020 8670 2525. Fax: 020 8761 6574
Email: fulltimemothers@hotmail.com
Web: www.fulltimemothers.org

Home Start
(*Offers the support of one volunteer parent to another parent
who is facing difficulties and has at least one child under five*)
2 Salisbury Road, Leicester, LE1 7QR
Tel: 0116 233 9955
Email: info@home start.org.uk
Web: www.home-start.org.uk

National Council for One-Parent Families
Tel: 0207 267 1361

National Family and Parenting Institute
(*Putting Families First*)
430 Highgate Road, London, NW5 1TL

Tel: 020 7424 3460. Fax: 020 7485 3590
Email: info@nfpi.org
Web: www.nfpi.org

National Parenting Centre
(*Guidance from child-rearing authorities*)
Web: www.tnpc.com

Parents Anonymous
(*Advice and help for parents having problems with their children*)
Tel: 0207 263 8918

Parent Lifeline (Helpline for Parents)
(*Provides the opportunity for parents (or carers) to talk about any problems or worries to a supportive listener who is also a parent*)
Volserve House, 14–18 West Bar Green, Sheffield, South Yorkshire, S1 2DA
Tel: 0114 272 6575
Email: office@parentlifeline.fsnet.co.uk

Parentline Plus
(*Incorporating Parentline and the National Step Family Association. Advice, information and support for parents and stepparents under stress*)
Tel: 0207 284 5500
Email: centraloffice@parentlineplus.org.uk

Parent Talk
(*Advice for parents*)
115 Southwark Bridge Road, London, SE1 0AX
Tel: 020 7450 9072/3. Fax: 020 7450 9060
Email: info@parentalk.co.uk
Web: www.parentalk.co.uk

Salvation Army (Home and Family Unit)
(*The Salvation Army is an integral part of the church involved in social and community action*)
101 Newington Causeway, London, SE1 6BN
Tel: 020 7367 4500. Fax: 020 7367 4711
Email: Judith.houghton@salvationarmy.org.uk
Web: www.salvationarmy.org.uk

Scottish Parenting Forum – Scotland
(*Aims to raise awareness of the needs of parents in Scotland and the widespread individual and social impact of parenting*)
Princes House, 5 Shandwick Place, Edinburgh, EH2 4RG
Tel: 0131 222 2420
Web: www.childreninscotland.org.uk/frame7.htm

The Parent Network
(*National network of local parent support groups, helping parents and children handle the ups and downs of family life*)
Tel: 01482 858 586

Young Minds
(*The Children's Mental Health Charity*)
102–108 Clerkenwell Road, London, EC1M 5SA
Tel: 020 7336 8445. Fax: 020 7336 8446
Parents Information Service: 0800 018 2138
Web: www.youngminds.org.uk

Your Parenting Lifeline Online
(*A list of charities, help organisations and support groups*)
Tel: 0191 260 2616. Fax: 0191 260 2636
Web: www.UKparents.co.uk

CADAS
(*Counselling service for alcoholism and drugs*)
Email: info@cadas.co.uk
Web: www.cadas.co.uk

Carlisle (Head Office): 1 Fisher Street, Carlisle,
CA3 8RR
Tel: 01228 544140 (Answerphone service)
Tel: 01228 599684. Fax: 01228 599684

West Cumbria
Tel: 01228 544140

Penrith: South Room, North Friargate, Penrith,
CA11 7XR
Tel: 01768 895566 (Answerphone redirect service)

Kendal: Stricklandgate House, 92 Stricklandgate,
Kendal, LA9 4PU
Tel: 01539 724772 (Answerphone)

Ulverston and South Lakes: Contact Kendal
(Answerphone redirect service)

GamCare
(*Advice on gambling problems*)
GamCare, Suite1, 25–27 Catherine Place, Westminster,
London, SW1E 6DU
Tel: 020 7233 8988. Fax: 020 7233 8977
Advice line: 0845 6000 133
Email: info@gamcare.org.uk
Web: www.GamCare.org.uk

Kidscape
2 Grosvenor Gardens, London, SW1W 0DH
Tel: 020 7730 3300. Fax: 020 7730 7081
Local rate tel: 08451 205204

Email for parents and professionals who have direct
experience of instigating an anti-bullying policy and
would like to share their thoughts with others:
Experience@kidscape.org.uk
Email for enquiries: webinfo@kidscape.org.uk

Pregnancy, Parenting & Motherhood Index
Tel: 01453 768160. Fax: (+44) 01285 740540
Email: Ruth@ridethemagiccarpet.co.uk
Web: www.ridethemagiccarpet.co.uk

IRELAND

Cherish
(*Advice information and support for single parents*)
2 Lower Pembroke Street, Dublin 2
Tel: (01) 662 9212

Gingerbread
(*Association for one-parent families*)
29 Dame Street, Dublin 2
Tel: (01) 671 0291

Parentline
(*Organisation for parents under stress*)
Carmichael House, North Brunswick Street, Dublin 2
Tel: (01) 873 3500

Parenting Forum NI (Northern Ireland)
(*The Parenting Forum NI aims to raise awareness of
parenting and its impact on the holistic development of
children through their lives and life stages*)
C/o Parents Advice Centre, Franklin House,
12 Brunswick Street, Belfast, BT7 7GE
Tel: 028 9031 0891
Email: pacbelfast@dnet.co.uk
Web: www.d-n-a.net/users/pacbelfast/parforum.html

USA

Parenting Concerns
Tel: 001 (408) 279 8228

Whole Family.Com
(*Share support with professionals and other parents*)
Web: www.wholefamily.com

AUSTRALIA

Counselling Services for Parents and Children
Web: www.aifs.org.au/nch/nchhelp.html

AUSTRALIAN CAPITAL TERITORY

Parent Line
(*Provides a statewide telephone support service*)
Tel: (02) 13 2055 – can only be dialled within Australia

QUEENSLAND

Parentline
(*A confidential telephone counselling service for parents and/
or primary care givers*)
PO Box 376, Red Hill, Queensland 4059.
(Counselling line for the cost of a local call, 8 a.m.–10 p.m.
7 days)
Tel: 00 61(07) 3858 5371; 1300 0 1300.
Fax: 00 61(07) 3367 1266
Email: parentline@kidshelp.com.au
Web: www.parentline.com.au

Partners in Parenting
(*A family support program providing counselling*)
PO Box 501, Wynnum, Queensland 4178
Tel: 00 61(07) 3393 5088. Fax: 00 61(07) 3393 5080

Parent Help Line
(*Child and Youth Health Parent helpline provides telephone
information, counselling and support*)
Tel: 00 61(08) 1300 364 100

VICTORIA

Parentline
(*Provides a telephone advisory and information service for
parents and children in Victoria as well as providing a
helpline, the service also offers a TTY (teletypewriter)
service for those with hearing difficulties*)
Tel: 00 61(03) 13 2289. TTY Service: 00 61(03) 13 6388

WESTERN AUSTRALIA

Parent line
(*Provides a telephone service for parenting information and
advice*)
Tel: 00 61(08) 9272 146

Useful websites

There are literally hundreds of good websites for parents
and families that are packed with useful information and
links. The following are a few places to start:

www.rollercoaster.ie
An excellent Irish-based resource, full of useful articles,
bulletin boards and links. Also sends out a regular news-
letters to subscribers.

www.solo.ie
A popular Irish-based website for single parents.

www.gingerbread.co.uk
UK-based website for single parents.

www.parentline.co.uk
UK website with a range of useful parenting information.

www.parenting.sa.gov.au
This website is an initiative of the Government of South
Australia designed to promote the value of parents and to
improve the quality of parenting.

www.parenting.org
A well-organised parenting website set up by a non-profit
child care organisation in America.

www.parenthoodweb.com
General American parenting website.

www.child.com
Website associated with the American magazine *Child*.

Further reading

Cohen, D. (2001) *The Father's Book. Being a Good Dad in the 21st
    Century*. Chichester: John Wiley & Sons.
Coleman, J. (2001) *Sex and Your Teenager: A Parent's Guide*.
    Chichester: John Wiley & Sons.
Covey, S. R. (1997) *The Seven Habits of Highly Effective Families*.
    London: Simon & Schuster.
Dinkmeyer, D., and D. G. McKay (1982) *STEP: Systematic Training
    for Effective Parenting*. Random House.
Forehand, R., and N. Long (1996) *Parenting the Strong-willed Child*.
    Chicago: Contemporary Books.
Gottman, J. (1997) *The Heart of Parenting*. London: Bloomsbury.

Gordon, T. (1975) *PET: Parent Effectiveness Training*. New York: Penguin.

Green, C. (1992) *Toddler Taming*. London: Vermillion.

Nelson, J., and L. Lott (2000) *Positive Discipline for Teenagers*. Roseville, California: Prima Publishing.

Quinn, M., and T. Quinn (1988) *What Can a Parent of a Teenager Do?* Newry: Family Caring Trust.

Quinn, M., and T. Quinn (1995) *What Can a Parent Do? The Five to Fifteen Basic Parenting Programme*. Belfast: Family Caring Trust.

Webster-Stratton, C. (1992) *The Incredible Years: A Trouble Shooting Guide for Parents of Children Aged 3–8*. Ontario: Umbrella Press.

Sharry, J. (2001) *When Parents Separate: A Guide to Helping Your Children Cope*. Dublin: Veritas.

For group leaders

Sharry, J., and C. Fitzpatrick (1997) *Parents Plus Progamme: A video-based guide to managing and solving discipline problems in children aged 4–11*. Parents Plus, c/o Mater Child Guidance Clinic, Mater Hospital, North Circular Road, Dublin 7.

Sharry, J. and C. Fitzpatrick (2001) *Parents Plus Families and Adolescents Progamme: A video-based guide to managing conflict and getting on better with older children and teenagers aged 11–16*. Parents Plus, c/o Mater Child Guidance Clinic, Mater Hospital, North Circular Road, Dublin 7.
www.brieftherapy.ie/parentsplus

Index

FAMILY MATTERS SERIES

Also Available in This Series

Toddler Troubles
coping with your under 5s
0-470-84686-0

Having it All?
choices for today's superwoman
0-470-84687-9

Sex and Your Teenager
a parent's guide
0-471-48562-4

The Father's Book
being a good dad in the 21st century
0-470-84133-8

Living Happily Ever After
putting reality into your romance
0-470-84134-6

Postnatal Depression
facing the paradox of loss,
happiness and motherhood
0-471-48527-6

Available from all good booksellers or to order direct:

DIAL FREE (UK only) 0800 243407 or (for overseas) · 44 (0) 1243 843294 or
fax · 44 (0) 1243 770677 or email: cs-books@wiley.co.uk

John Wiley & Sons, Ltd, The Atrium, Southern Gate, Chichester, PO19 8SQ

www.wileyeurope.com

 WILEY

3318a